THE
CORE
PREPARED WARRIORS

Life's is hard, but there is a way to find
peace in the midst of life's battles.
Connect to the Core and you will endure.

Crystal Campbell

THE CORE

Cover and interior design by Crystal Campbell
Cover photo by Kevin Carden – stock.adobe.com
Edited by James Wagner

THE CORE

Copyright © 2020 Crystal Campbell
Published by Crystal Campbell
Brentwood, California 94513
www.preparedwarriors.com

LCCN   2020915339
ISBN   978-1-7355618-0-6
eISBN   978-1-7355618-1-3

Printed in the United States of America

DEDICATION

It is with the greatest and deepest appreciation, I dedicate this book to my family, who are all warriors in their own right: Corey, Sadie, Teyo, Sophia, Nia, Dad, Mom, Angie, Beckie, David, and Ellie. You have each overcome many of life's battles and never gave up! You inspire me. May God bless each of you with a household of faithful Prepared Warriors for generations to come, and may it begin with you.

Special thanks to my sister, Angie, who as a child, in an effort to shut down my talkative nature, would say, "just go write it in your book." Thank you for the prophetic declaration you spoke over me again and again. It has finally come to pass.

THANKS

All thanks and praise to God the Father, Son, and Holy Spirit. You have been my precious Savior all my life. You never left me, even in the hardest moments. You carried me through the pain and refined me in your fire. I finally emerged from that dark season. Then, you showed me that drawing closer to you, through your Word, worship, and prayer, was a strategy for victory you wanted me to share. So, Prepared Warriors was born. You had me step out of my comfort zone and start live broadcasts and start writing my first book, The Core. Every time I cried out to you, "help me write the truth God," you proved yourself faithful. You're amazing. God, your plans are always right. May you be glorified through every word of this book and ministry.

Thank you to my Editor, James Wagner, for graciously agreeing to work with me on my first book. To my lifelong friend and prayer partner, Dionne, who also happens to be an amazing proofreader, thank you! Thank you to all of my beta readers for your feedback that made every bit better. Thank you to my dear friends who faithfully prayed for me every step of the way: Dove, Edwina, Christina, Angie, Vicki, Connilyn, and Lisa. I LOVE YOU! I would also like to thank all my friends who contributed to the publishing of this book. I'm so thankful for each of you, your support, and encouragement.

Finally, I would like to thank my husband, Corey, for believing in me, and encouraging me as I wrote this book. Your love has saved us over and over, "love never fails." (1 Corinthians 13:8) Thank you to my beautiful children, Sadie, Teyo, Sophia, and Nia, who listened to me read so much of what I wrote. I love you each dearly and pray daily for you to become strong Prepared Warriors. Thank you to my parents who raised me to be a warrior with a foundation of faith in the one true living God.

THE CORE

C O N T E N T

PROLOGUE

As the dust rises above the battle, the war rages on. Fierce warriors fighting side by side with young fresh warriors. The enemy cares not the rank of soldier, its only mission is to destroy. Think not that this war is optional. No reprieve will be given. The immense weight of the season is upon us. The hour is late. The time is now. Will you rise, or will you fall? Your preparation makes all the difference. Have you prepared for this moment? Do you know your weapons? Can you swing your sword? Do you carry a shield? The moment you step on the battlefield every weakness is amplified and readily visible to the enemy and you. Now as each warrior fights for their lives, they must also gather their armor at the same time. Piecing together their covering even as the enemy slings its arrows and crushes down on them. Some warriors struggle and others come to help, but they are also under attack and cannot possibly assist each other enough to dissuade the enemy from their demise. They must stand. They must fight. They must.

All around us spiritual wars rage on: sickness, relationship problems, mental health, political upheaval, sin abounds, families crumble. Yet in the midst of the chaos, in the heart of the storm is you. You are silently watching the world swirl around you, yet you have peace that passes all understanding. The storm does not overtake you. You stand strong, confident, unmoved by the flurry of debris that threatens to strike you.

How? How does this happen? Why are there those who come through tragedy, or trials unscathed? They emerge with gems of wisdom and knowledge, with a peaceful spirit. They, you, have something, a secret weapon, a power that eclipses any storm, any weapon, any enemy. It is so simple many miss it. They overlook it and pass it up as outdated or irrelevant. But you know the truth. The truth has set you free. The truth is you are connected to the Core. The Core of all creation. The Core of all people. The source of all life. The source of love, joy, peace, patience, kindness, goodness, faithfulness, gentleness, and self-control.

You have a steady flow of the life-giving energy, the wisdom of the universe, and the perspective of Heaven. You carry the Core within you, and draw from this power, wisdom, and love daily. It fills you and provides for your every need. It prepares you for every battle. It allows you to see what it sees. It protects you. You are surrounded by favor and blessings even while the enemy attacks you with all its might. The Core. The Core is the key. You must have the Core and connect with it continually. It is the only way to survive and remain at peace. The Core is God – the Father, Son, and Holy Spirit.

It is possible to know about God and not have the Core. It is possible to believe in Jesus and not have the Core. It is even possible to have the Holy Spirit and not reap the blessings of Core connection. The Core connection is where all of the power lies. It is where the peace, love, healing, and acceptance lies. Sporadic spurts or occasional dips in the spring of life cannot possibly sustain you in battle. A continual flow and exchange must be established and fostered to receive the full blessing, favor, and gifts from the Core. Once your connection is secure, and you begin to receive all of the goodness of God, you will not want to turn it off! You will, "Taste and see that the Lord is good; blessed is the one who takes refuge in him." (Psalm 34:8)

Time is pressing. There is no moment to waste. Seize the daylight while it lasts. (John 9:4) Connect to the Core, connect to God and receive all you can now. For a time will soon be upon us when darkness rises and the time to prepare is over. Heed the parable of the Ten Virgins. Only five of them were prepared when the bridegroom arrived. The other five were left behind because they were not prepared.

> *But while they were on their way to buy the oil, the bridegroom arrived. The virgins who were ready went in with him to the wedding banquet. And the door was shut. - Matthew 25:10*

We are sounding the alarm and calling all warriors to PREPARE for battle. The time is now. Where do we begin? How can we possibly prepare for the days to come? Maybe you are already under attack and struggling to just survive. No matter where you find yourself, no matter what age, experience, or stage, we must all prepare.

Nothing happens by accident. You reading this book is not an accident. God has a plan and purpose for you. The creator of the entire universe wants YOU to be a part of His kingdom.

You may not believe in God, or know who Jesus is. We will go over exactly who He is, and why He is an essential part for your victory. But first, I must give a warning. The devil does not like people to know the truth. He will try to stop you from preparing. He will speak as though a thought in your own mind. Do not believe his lies. Jesus tells us about Satan, "… there is no truth in him. When he lies, he speaks his native language, for he is a liar and the father of lies." (John 8:44) Satan's lies are meant to keep you out of Heaven and send you to hell, plain and simple. You might hear or think…

"No one really cares what I do, or if I even exist"
TRUTH: God made you for a purpose. He made you and He doesn't make mistakes. "I praise you because I am fearfully and wonderfully made; your works are wonderful; I know that full well." (Psalm 139:14)

"I've done too many bad things. God can't use me now."

TRUTH: The blood of Jesus is more powerful than your sin. He can use even the hardest things you have been through for His good and glory. Many people are able to help other people through what they have experienced themselves. "And we know that in all things God works for the good of those who love him, who have been called according to his purpose." (Romans 8:28)

"I don't believe there is a god."

TRUTH: There is a God. He is very real. He reveals Himself in His creation all around you. "For since the creation of the world God's invisible qualities – his eternal power and divine nature – have been clearly seen, being understood from what has been made, so that people are without excuse." (Romans 1:20)

"God doesn't love me."

TRUTH: God loves you so much more than you could ever imagine. He loves you so much that He allows you to choose Him. He doesn't force you to love Him. Even before we loved him, He gave His life, so our sins could be forgiven. "But God demonstrated his own love for us in this: While we were still sinners, Christ died for us." (Romans 5:8)

"I don't have time to figure all this out. I'm too busy right now."

TRUTH: None of us are promised tomorrow. Your eternal destiny and purpose are too important to put off! Ultimately, you make time for what is important to you. You may not be in the midst of the storm now, but storms are sure to come. If you prepare now, you will be able to withstand the storm, and live victorious. Remember, "you know very well that the day of the Lord will come like a thief in the night." (1 Thessalonians 5:2) Be ready.

**"I've been Christian all my life, I already know
all I need to know about God, and the Bible."**

TRUTH: None of us know all there is to know about God and the Bible. "How great is God – beyond our understanding!" (Job 36:26) We should be continuingly growing and learning. A great prayer is, "God help me learn more about you and how your Kingdom works."

**"Every age there is someone saying it's the tribulation period.
I don't need to prepare, because it isn't happening in my lifetime."**

TRUTH: We all need to prepare because Jesus told us He would return, "But about that day or hour no one knows, not even the angels in heaven, not the Son, but only the Father." (Matthew 24:36) If Christ returned today could you say all your accounts are in order, you fulfilled all He planned for you, and you are ready to meet your Maker

**"I'm getting raptured any day now.
I won't have to go through any tribulation."**
TRUTH: Rapture or not, Christians are already being persecuted and martyred around the world at alarming rates. There are many Christian ministries that track and report this specific information. We cannot count on a pre-tribulation Rapture, even if the best and brightest prophecy scholars believe it.

There are other amazing prophecy scholars who believe we will go through the tribulation period. Many modern-day Prophets are on a mission to help prepare Christians to endure through the tribulation period. Eventually we will all know who was right. But, wouldn't it be wise to prepare to endure through persecution and the tribulation period?

We simply don't have enough space in this book to debunk every lie the enemy speaks. Just note that it is his voice, not yours, and it's not true. You don't have to agree with it. Do not be distracted, discouraged, become complacent, or be tempted to stop reading. This book is important because it shows you how to connect to the truth that will set you free, give you victory, and eternal life in Heaven. That's a pretty large claim! This book alone is not that powerful, but it points you to the one who is, and shows you how to connect to Him. God, the Core, is the key to everything.

PART 1
MASTERS &
ALLEGIANCE

Chapter 1

TJ'S STORY
CHOOSE A SIDE

"How was school today TJ?" He gave his standard reply, "Normal." But, today was anything but normal. There was a war raging within his soul. He would not be able to rest until it was all settled. His entire paradigm had shifted in one conversation.

The demons were doing their best to fly interference and keep TJ from even meeting the Christian boy, Teyo, the warrior. But the warrior's angels were strong and fierce. He moved freely no matter how they tried to block him. There was little they could do when the warrior approached TJ. They screamed "Go away! Don't listen to him! He doesn't know what he's talking about! Run!" But TJ didn't leave, he started talking to the warrior! "Reinforcements!! We need reinforcements!!" But it was too late, the area was blocked off by angels now. Their numbers seemed to multiply in an instance, and the demons assigned to TJ cowered in their presence.

The boys made quick introductions; they had never met before. As they discussed their various groups and activities, Teyo asked "So, do you go to church anywhere? Are you a Christian?" That threw TJ off guard. He didn't know how to give a simple answer. His family used to attend a church, but when they moved, they never found a new church, and he had kind of forgotten about it. Teyo proceeded to tell him about his church and invited TJ to attend with him.

The demons continued to protest, "I told you to run! Never listen to a Christian! They don't even like you! They just try to sell you their religion! It's awful! He's a liar! Run away!" But the angels stood their ground and the warrior's protection was secure with the seal of God on him. He was untouchable, but TJ wasn't. They focused their attention on TJ. He must listen to them; they have become good friends. He always listened to them before. What was wrong with him?

The exchange was rather quick, but before they parted Teyo asked one last question, "Hey TJ, if you died today, do you know for sure where you would go?" TJ wasn't sure about anything. He didn't even understand his math homework. But he did know that was an important question, even for someone his age. Before he moved, a classmate, he knew well, died. It seemed surreal, but he knew it was all too real. Death does happen, even for young people. He wanted what Teyo seemed to have, a peace about life and death. It didn't appear to scare him at all. As he walked away, he knew this would occupy his mind until he had the answer.

That night TJ went to bed early. He had so much to think about. Even as he thought, the demons assigned to him began to speak again, "You don't have to think about this now. You're young, you're not going to die. You've got plenty of time to figure this out. Just go to sleep, you're so tired." But even as they spoke, TJ knew it wasn't true. He knew the truth, that none of us know when our time is up. He knew it was important because he could feel the empty pit in his stomach confirming the need, the desire for more.

Just then, an angel stepped into the room. The demon shrieked, "You can't come in here! This is my territory! You have no right to be here! Get away from him! He's mine!" But the angel did not budge and moved without even acknowledging the demon. As the demon threw his tantrum, resisting, and shrieking with all his might, he didn't notice the light that entered the room. The light of the Holy Spirit came down softly and gently rested right on TJ's heart.

TJ sensed a change in the atmosphere. He was so agitated before, but now he relaxed, and began to think clearly. He didn't know what would happen to his soul when he dies. That was clear. He knew where he wanted to go, Heaven. But he was not clear on how that gets decided. Who decides? What do I need to do? What is my part in all of this? He decided to write down his questions and find the Christian boy again tomorrow.

But tomorrow turned into the next day, and the next day, and days and days. First TJ got sick. The demon brought in his buddy Sickness, to keep TJ in bed until he forgot about this heaven foolishness. Then, when TJ started feeling better, he made sure TJ was preoccupied with extra homework, lots of sports, a new video game, his phone, and activities. He would just make sure he was too busy to think about heaven or remember the warrior.

Days turned into weeks, but TJ did not forget. In fact, it only increased his longing for answers. TJ eventually decided to ask his mom if she had a Bible. He could read it himself and find the answers. It had been a long time since she had used it and she wasn't able to find it. Then, he thought about searching online. There was a lot of information about Jesus and heaven, but TJ didn't know what the truth was and what he could trust. He knew the Warrior, Teyo, had the truth, it was written all over his confident presence. But he didn't seem to cross paths with him again.

In that moment, TJ decided to speak to Jesus for the first time, "Jesus if you're real, would you reveal yourself to me? Help me find out about heaven and how to get there." That simple prayer elicited a roaring response in the spirit realm! Shouts of praise, and victory came from the angels, "May God be praised! Prepare the way for a new soul! He is seeking you Christ! Glory to God!!" But the demons began to shriek in agony and defeat, "No! Not another one! He was defeated already! He belonged to me." But TJ did not belong to the demons. He never did.

The next day as TJ walked to class, his mind was on his math assignment, when someone shouted his name from down the hall. He turned around to see Teyo! After all this time! TJ had looked for him each day for so long, and today Teyo finds him! Did God hear his prayer? TJ wasted no time, "Hey I've been doing a lot of thinking since our last talk. Could we maybe hang out later? I've got some questions for you." "Sounds good," Teyo responded.

The boys did meet later. As they met, their angels came together in joy and excitement. They knew the contents of the meeting would honor God, and possibly elicit a new soul for the kingdom of God. As the boys talked, more angels joined the gathering. The excitement and joy were contagious. Then, Teyo began to share the gospel message of Jesus Christ. Shouts of "Amen!" and "Hallelujah!" erupted from the witnesses. The celebration continued until all at once, every eye looked up. There from the clouds, the Spirit of God, began to slowly descend. All at once, the angels let out a collective shout, "Glory to God most High! Holy, Holy, Holy are You!"

Teyo was so prepared, he brought his Bible and showed TJ how Jesus Christ died for his sins. He told TJ, "Just tell Jesus you know you have sinned, and you need Him. Ask Him to be Lord of your life."

TJ did just that. As he prayed the Holy Spirit, that had rested on his heart, moved into his heart. At that moment, the demons who were causing TJ such trouble before, came out with shrieks of pain. They could no longer dwell with TJ, because the Holy Spirit had claimed him. The light of the Lord enveloped TJ like a warm blanket from the inside out. Shouts of joy erupted from the angels who had gathered. What a celebration!! There were beams of light shooting in every direction! Shouts of joy and excitement! Another soul was won for the Kingdom of God!! Hallelujah!!

TJ, though unaware of the great celebration in the spirit realm, immediately felt different. A warm feeling came over him like a blanket. He felt lighter, cleaner, clearer, and he was filled with a peaceful feeling. He knew he would remember that feeling the rest of his life.

Chapter 2

MASTERS & ALLEGIANCE

Becoming a Prepared Warrior starts here. The entry point for your journey begins with choosing where your allegiance lies, and what master you will serve. Make no mistake, we all choose a side and serve a master consciously, or unconsciously. So, what is a master? You may have heard Jesus referred to by his disciples as "Master." Some highly respected teachers are referred to as "master" by their students. According to Merriam-Webster Dictionary, Master has many meanings, the most fitting being, "one having authority over another: Ruler, Governor," and "Having chief authority: Dominant." Who or what rules your life and your decisions?

In any given situation there can only be one master. It is true that, "No one can serve two masters. Either you will hate the one and love the other, or you will be devoted to one and despise the other." (Luke 16:13) The master you choose to serve determines the decisions you make, how you spend your time and money, your allegiance, what side you are on, and where you will spend eternity. Who or what is your master?

The good news is you get to choose your master. Yes, it is a big decision. The biggest, most important decision in your life. Yet, there are few occasions in life when you are faced with the reality of this choice. Not often in the midst of our busy days do we consider the afterlife, or the decisions we must make that will determine our eternal status. Our days are too busy, and our minds too preoccupied to stop for such deep contemplation. Thus, most people fall into unconsciously choosing money or work as their master, they may choose themselves and their own pleasure as their master, their self-identity, political or social group as their master, or even their friends or family may become their master. Of all of the possible masters we could choose, once we remove all the filters and come down to the very bottom line of it all, your choice is God or Satan.

When provided the general understanding of God and Satan, most people would reject Satan if he came to us in his pure evil form. But Satan is deceptive, tempting, and entices people with any number of weapons:

comfort, greed, selfishness, vanity, pride, lust, addictions, self-identity, self-righteousness, religious spirits ... I could go on and on. Satan may have already tried to violently claim you through abuse, destruction, violence, etc. But he doesn't get to choose, you do. The choice between God and Satan is very real and holds eternal consequences. Choosing God as your master means eternity in heaven. But, if you do not choose God as your master, you default to Satan and will spend eternity in hell. No one wants that, or consciously chooses hell. But it is the absolute truth. Let me explain.

Think of yourself as a house. Your house is filled with all kinds of stuff, things you love, things you hate, things you hold onto because they help define who you are, and also loads of trash (sin). Some people's houses are a mess, overflowing with debris and clearly in need of some major help. Some people's homes look nice on the outside, and may even have a clean clear surface to impress their guests. But, even if you made it look nice on the outside, there is no way you can clean the inside on your own. Everyone has at least one room no one can enter. It holds all your skeletons, secrets, sins, things you'd rather not think about, and certainly don't want anyone to see. Now, what you need to know is that Satan has already assumed rights to your home, as the owner or master.

His minions, AKA demons, are already hanging out. If you open the door to him, he comes in and invites all his nasty friends to come into your house too. But the amazing thing is, Jesus, whether you believe in Him or not, has already purchased your home. In fact, he paid way more for it than your house is worth! He covered all the cost. Though He is the owner and master, He is a gentleman and will not take-over ownership without your permission. That's right, you have to accept the agreement, because it is legally binding. If you accept Jesus's ownership and allow him to become master over your home, the devil and his friends will be evicted from the premises. Then, the fun begins.

God moves in and starts to remodel your home. He is a great designer and remodeler. You see He actually built your home, "God is the builder of everything," and knows exactly how it is supposed to look and function. (Hebrews 3:4) But, again He is a gentleman, patient, and full of grace. He will go room by room, piece by piece and examine the contents of your home. He will say "Let's look at this old couch (an old wound or hurt). It has holes in it. Would you like to get rid of it? I'll get you a new one." If you keep saying yes to God, He will keep making your home better and better. Some people are brave and consent to a full remodeling process right away. They repent, forgive, and release anger, pain and bitterness. This can be painful and a lot of work, but the end result is glorious and takes way less time than going bit by bit.

As we discussed, there are some rooms and areas of your house that may be off limits. You may have decided to ignore it, push it in the corner, and not allow anyone in. But God already knows every part of your house. He sees every nook and cranny. He already knew about your secret room before He purchased your house, and He bought it anyway. It does you no good to hold onto that room. The designer will open the door and slowly remove all the junk, piece by piece, until the room is empty. It can be swept and cleaned.

If you watch design shows on tv, you have probably seen people who think they know better than the designer. It's frustrating to watch because we know they always end up messing things up, and frustrating the designer. The designer is the master. You have to consciously accept Him as your master, let go and trust God. He knows what He is doing.

Allow God to fully clean, remodel, and upgrade your house. Then your home will look and feel so wonderful, bright, open, and free. You'll gladly have friends over, gladly share what you have, gladly tell others about your designer and master. Once you let Him just do what He does best, and get out of His way, your home becomes glorious. You become glorious.

THE CORE

20

Chapter 3

SATAN OR GOD

Who will you allow to own and live in your house, God or Satan? That decision determines if you will go to Heaven or Hell. There are no other places, no other options for us after we die. You either go to Heaven or Hell. There is no evidence for rebirth, dying into nothingness, or going to planets filled with virgins. Yet, there are thousands of cases of people who have had near death experiences and come back to tell the tales of Heaven and Hell. So, let's compare your options:

Some words used to describe Satan are:
- seeking to devour (1 Peter 5:8)
- murderer & father of lies (John 8:44)
- dragon, ancient serpent, deceiver (Revelation 12:9)
- thief who comes only to steal and kill and destroy (John 10:10)
- accuser of our brothers (Revelation 12:9-12)
- the evil one (1 John 5:19)

> *But woe to the earth and the sea, because the devil has gone down to you! He is filled with fury, because he knows that his time is short. - Revelation 12:12*

Satan is not your friend. He wants nothing good for you. His plan is for you to go to hell. No one really wants to go to hell except true Satan worshipers. Satan promises them they will rule and reign in hell. He lied about that too. Didn't we already find out that Satan is a liar? Yes, He is the father of lies. They will not rule, reign or enjoy any aspect of Hell. Hell is eternal torture.

Hell is widely understood to be a terrible place. In some instances, people make light of it, and imagine in their minds that it is an eternal party for all of the sinners and "fun people." That's not at all how the Bible describes it. It says, "... The angels will come and separate the wicked from the righteous and throw them into the blazing furnace, where there will be weeping and gnashing of teeth." (Matthew 13: 49-50) It is truly more awful than we can imagine. The complete absence of God and all aspects of the Kingdom of God will leave only utter darkness and despair. It is said, "He will punish those who do not know God and do not obey the gospel of our Lord Jesus. They will be punished with everlasting destruction and shut out from the presence of the Lord and from the glory of his might." (2 Thessalonians 1:8-9) There is no party; instead there is punishment with everlasting destruction.

Another lie Satan tries to propagate is that there is no hell, or that it was made up by the Catholic church to keep people under their control. While the Catholic church has a sordid history of abuses and lies, hell most assuredly is not a lie. Hell is backed up in scripture, and Jesus himself spoke Matthew 13:49-50. Jesus continues to warn us, "And if your eye causes you to sin, pluck it out. It is better for you to enter the kingdom of God with one eye than to have two eyes and be thrown into hell, where 'their worm does not die, and the fire is not quenched.' Everyone will be salted with fire." (Mark 9:47-49) Hell is awful; it's terrible.

Hell is the reason Christians try so desperately to share the good news of Jesus. We don't want anyone to spend eternity in Hell and neither does Jesus, "...(Jesus) is patient with you, not wanting anyone to perish, but everyone to come to repentance." (2 Peter 3:9) The Apostle Paul was commissioned by Jesus who said, "I am sending you to them to open their eyes and turn them from darkness to light, and from the power of Satan to God, so that they may receive forgiveness of sins and a place among those who are sanctified by faith in me." (Acts 26:17-18)

So now let's talk about God. The term "God" encompasses the holy Trinity: God the Father, the Son (Jesus), and the Holy Spirit. God is three parts in one being, similar to humans being made up of three parts (mind, body, and spirit) united within one being. We will discuss this more thoroughly in the Core connection chapter.

Words used to describe God are:
- Father (1 Peter 1:2)
- King (Psalm 10:16)
- Master (Colossians 4:1)
- Creator (Genesis 1:1)
- Lord (Philippians 2:11)
- Healer (Exodus 15:26)
- Provider (Romans 8:32)
- Good Shepherd (Matthew 18:12-14)
- Savior (Luke 1:47)
- Peace (Judges 6:22-24)

- Love (1 John 4:16)
- Faithful (Deuteronomy 7:9)
- Merciful (Deuteronomy 4:31)
- Gracious (Psalm 116:5)
- Patient (2 Peter 3:9)
- Forgiving (Matthew 26:28)
- Kind (Romans 2:4)
- Redeemer (Psalm 78:35)
- Judge (Psalm 7:11)
- Lord of Hosts (Commander of angel armies Psalm 103:21)
- Almighty, All-Sufficient God (Ephesians 1:19-21)
- Everlasting God (Psalm 90:2)
- Righteousness (Jeremiah 23:5-6
- Sanctifies (Exodus 31:12-13)

God is so much more amazing and complex than who we create Him to be in our minds. The Bible gives us so many great words that describe God, but most importantly we are given story after story that demonstrates His character. We can see for ourselves how Jesus responded to sinners, or how God dealt with the sin and rebellion of the Israelites.

We see how patient He was with them giving ample opportunities to turn from sin, repent and come to Him. We also see that He is the great Judge, who is the only omniscient, righteous and holy being. He is this amazing combination of loving and strong, full of grace and loves justice. God is truly amazing. The more you learn and know about God the more you want to spend time with Him.

When we see the comparison between God and Satan, there really is no comparison. Jesus shows us the comparison clearly, "The thief comes only to steal and kill and destroy. I came that they may have life and have it abundantly." (John 10:10) God is the Core, the source for all goodness, love, peace, joy and so much more. Satan's main goal is to keep us separate from the Core, because <u>he himself is</u> separated from the Core.

Then war broke out in heaven. Michael and his angels fought against the dragon, and the dragon and his angels fought back. But he was not strong enough, and they lost their place in heaven. The great dragon was hurled down – that ancient serpent called the devil, or Satan, who leads the whole world astray. He was hurled to the earth, and his angels with him.
- Revelation 12:7-9

23

WHO DO YOU SAY JESUS IS?

There are a lot of people who believe there is a "God," and would say "I choose God." But they are not sure about Jesus. They aren't sure who He is or why He's important. Some say He is just a prophet, a teacher, or an angel. In Mark 8:27-30 Jesus asks Peter "Who do you say I am?" Peter answered, "You are the Messiah."

Jesus confirmed this again when on trial before the religious leaders, "The high priest said to him, 'I charge you under oath by the living God: Tell us if you are the Christ, the Son of God.' 'Yes, it is as you say,' Jesus replied. 'But I say to all of you: In the future you will see the Son of Man sitting at the right hand of the Mighty One and coming on the clouds of heaven." (Matthew 26:63-64)

The Messiah, the Christ, is the prophesied Son of God and Savior for all mankind. There are hundreds of prophecies in the Bible, written hundreds to a thousand years before Jesus was born. The prophecies tell where he will be born, what family line he will come from, what his ministry will be, his death and resurrection, and much more. Amazingly, <u>Jesus fulfilled EVERY SINGLE PROPHECY</u>. The mathematical probability of one man fulfilling all of these prophecies is 1×10^{17} power, as calculated in the book "Science Speaks" by noteworthy scholars Peter W. Stoner, M.S. and Robert C. Newman, S.T.M., Ph.D. Jesus truly is the Messiah, the Christ, the Son of God.

WHY IS JESUS SO IMPORTANT?

To put it simply, only Jesus has the power to save us, "Salvation is found in no one else, for there is no other name under heaven given to mankind by which we must be saved." (Acts 4:12) Jesus paid the price for our sins by dying on the cross. Just as Isaiah prophesied, "...he poured out his life unto death, and was numbered with the transgressors. For he bore the sin of many and made intercession for the transgressors." (Isaiah 53:12) Without Jesus's blood, our sins are not paid for. "For the wages of sin is death..." (Romans 6:23) Because of our sin, we should be subject to death. We know that, "All have sinned and fall short of the glory of God." (Romans 3:23) How can we possibly be righteous enough to enter the Kingdom of God?

Many religions center around working your way to Heaven, they believe you must earn it. But, Romans 6:23 goes on to say, "... but the gift of God is eternal life in Christ Jesus our Lord." Jesus is the good and perfect "gift of God" so we can have payment for our sins and spend eternal life in Heaven. "Whoever believes in the Son has eternal life, but whoever rejects the Son will not see life, for God's wrath remains on them." (John 3:36)

Scripture tells us that no one gets to God except through Jesus. Jesus is essential. He said, "I am the way and the truth and the life. <u>No one comes to the Father except through me.</u>" (John 14:6 emphasis added) Jesus was part of God's redemption plan from the very beginning, "For God so loved the world, that he gave his only Son, that whoever believes in him should not perish but have eternal life. For God did not send his Son into the world to condemn the world, but to save the world through him. Whoever believes in him is not condemned, but whoever does not believe stands condemned already because they have not believed in the name of God's one and only Son." (John 3:16-18) So, there is a very clear decision here. Believe in Jesus and be SAVED, or don't believe in Jesus and stand condemned. It truly is your own choice if you are condemned or saved.

God already chose you, "For my Father's will is that everyone who looks to the Son and believes in him shall have eternal life, and I will raise them up at the last days." (John 6:30) There was no qualification on the word "everyone". The scripture doesn't say only people who have committed no sins, or only the "good people" get to heaven. It doesn't say only people of a certain skin color, or only the wealthy. No, it says "EVERYONE who looks to the Son and believes in him shall have eternal life." That means you, no matter who you are, what you have done, where you came from, or where you are now. If you choose to look to the Son (Jesus) and believe in him, you shall have eternal life, "Whoever has the Son has life; whoever does not have the Son of God does not have life." (1 John 5:12)

Jesus' life reveals who He is. You can see for yourself by reading the gospels: Matthew, Mark, Luke, and John. When you compare Jesus's life to any other god, prophet, or spiritual leader, Jesus always comes out on top. He lived a sinless life. He had the authority to cast out demons. He performed miracles and healed people everywhere he went. He gave his life to save our lives. He rose from the dead and is the only one that conquered death. His tomb is empty! He's coming back again as a conquering King!

JESUS CHRIST'S RETURN

It's extremely important to remember that Jesus is coming back again. That is why we are preparing and what this whole book is about! Prepared Warriors, "Seek the Lord while he may be found; call on him while he is near." (Isaiah 55:6) How you prepare now, and who you choose now will determine if you **rejoice** or **mourn** at Christ's return.

REJOICE: "When the Son of Man comes in his glory, and all the angels with him, he will sit on his glorious throne. All the nations will be gathered before him, and he will separate the people one from another as a shepherd separates the sheep from the goats. He will put the sheep on his right and the goats on his left. Then the King will say to those on his right, 'Come, you who are blessed by my Father; take your inheritance, the kingdom prepared for you since the creation of the world.'" (Matthew 25:31-34)

MOURN: "Look, he is coming with the clouds, and every eye will see him, even those who pierced him; and all the peoples of the earth will mourn because of him." (Revelation 1:7)

Chapter 4

CHOOSE YOUR MASTER

CHOOSE VICTORY

The book of Revelation is filled with prophecies of the end times, yet to be fulfilled. When you read it, you find out who wins in the end. Spoiler alert.... IT'S GOD!! "And the devil, who deceived them, was thrown into the lake of burning sulfur, where the beast and the false prophet had been thrown. They will be tormented day and night forever and ever." (Revelation 20:10) Not only does God win at the very end, He has a perfect record of victory in every single battle! "If God is for us, who can be against us?" (Romans 8:31) That doesn't mean that bad things don't happen to Christians. It means that God can do amazing things in the midst of the trials and by the end of the story, He will work it all for good. Our perspective of our circumstances is limited, but His is not.

KINGDOM BENEFITS

There are a lot of perks, benefits, and blessings that come with being a follower of Christ. You get a personal relationship with the ruler of the entire universe. God is not some all-powerful, yet silent being, not at all! When you choose Christ, you get access to Him. This book, "The Core – Prepared Warriors" is all about tapping into and benefiting from this amazing reality. You will come to find this benefit to be beyond what you imagined or hoped for. God is so much more amazing than any of us give Him credit for, and more amazing than our limited faith will allow.

You become a child of God, "Yet to all who did receive him, to those who believed in his name, he gave the right to become children of God." (John 1:12) He is the Father, the good Father. He loves and cherishes you as His creation, as His child. "How great is the love the Father has lavished on us, that we should be called children of God! And that is what we are!" (1 John 3:1) He will never leave or forsake you. (Deuteronomy 31:6) He will never abuse or mistreat you. He is full of love; "God is love." (1 John 4:8) He will correct and redirect you, as any truly good Father would, "Because the Lord disciplines those he loves, as a father the son delights in." (Proverbs 3:12) Discipline is a blessing because He doesn't allow you to fall into sin, falling further and further from Him. You belong to Him, and He will fight for you and protect you. You are a child of the King!

You become a part of the family of God. There are Christians all over the world. When the Spirit of God lives in you, and you meet someone else with that same Spirit there is an immediate connection and bond. We truly are a family. It is important to note the presence of the Spirit of God, and the fruit of the Spirit, discussed later in this chapter. There are many who claim to be Christians, but do not have the Spirit of God within them or display the fruit of the Spirit. You must use wisdom and discernment to see who the true family of God is. Once you do, there is great joy. You can build each other up, encourage one another, pray for each other. Amazing lifelong bonds are formed within the family of God.

Your sins are forgiven, "as far as the east is from the west, so far has he removed our transgressions from us." (Psalm 103:12) There are so many people who walk around weighted down by their sins. But, when you accept Jesus, His blood pays the price for the forgiveness of your sins. "He is the atoning sacrifice for our sins, and not only for ours but also for the sins of the whole world." (1 John 2:2) You can confess your sins and the Bible tells us, "he is faithful and just and will forgive us our sins and purify us from all unrighteousness." (1 John 1:9). I don't know about you, but that sounds so freeing. To release all of the sins of the past and let them go unshackles us and sets us free.

There is a beautiful story in Luke 7 about a sinful woman who washes Jesus' feet with her tears and her hair in such love and gratitude for His forgives. Jesus told his disciples, "I tell you, her many sins have been forgiven – as her great love has shown. But whoever has been forgiven little loves little." (Luke 7:47) Forgiveness is so amazing because it comes from God, the only one who truly has the power to forgive our sins. At the same time, He is the holiest, most righteous being. He has authority and every right to judge us according to His own laws. Yet when we humble ourselves and repent, He chooses mercy, grace, and forgiveness. It's such an amazing gift.

HEAVEN!!! Choosing Christ means eternity in Heaven instead of Hell. Heaven is also beyond our imagination but by all accounts, in the Bible it is glorious. Let's not allow our limited imaginations to diminish the awesomeness of Heaven. Every person who has had a near death experience and glimpsed Heaven has been amazed. Sin is not allowed in Heaven; it cannot dwell in the presence of God. Demons aren't allowed in Heaven either. So, we won't have to constantly war against the enemy, like we do on earth.

There are angels in heaven, and other amazing beings created by God. God himself resides in Heaven, "Heaven is my throne, and the earth is my footstool." (Isaiah 66:1) The glorious display of His splendor is quite simply unimaginable, but we get a glimpse in Revelation 4:1-6, "After this I looked, and there before me was a door standing open in heaven... there before me was a throne in heaven with someone sitting on it. And the one who sat there had the appearance of jasper and ruby. A rainbow that shone like an emerald encircled the throne. Surrounding the throne were twenty-four other thrones, and seated on them were twenty-four elders. They were dressed in white and had crowns of gold on their heads. From the throne came flashes of lightning, rumblings and peals of thunder. In front of the throne, seven lamps were blazing. These are the seven spirits of God. Also, in front of the throne there was what looked like a sea of glass, clear as crystal." Heaven holds so many blessings, but the most amazing aspect of Heaven will undoubtedly be beholding God Almighty on His throne.

You receive the Holy Spirit, God's Spirit, to dwell within you. The Spirit of God is amazing. His Spirit comes and dwells within His believers, and allows us to communicate with God, and God to communicate with us. Jesus said, "... the Helper, the Holy Spirit, whom the Father will send in my name, he will teach you all things and bring to your remembrance all that I have said to you." (John 14:26) The Holy Spirit is our comforter, our counselor, He gives us gifts, power, peace, joy, and so much more. Yes, the Core connection is connecting to the Holy Spirit. He is the source of everything we need to be Prepared Warriors.

You receive the fruit to the Spirit as you allow the Holy Spirit to rule and reign within you. When this happens the fruit of the Spirit will grow too. Like a tree bears fruit of the type of tree it is, so we bear fruit of the type of Spirit we have. If you allow your own spirit to rule you, you may have good days, and bad days. You may be nice or mean. You may be selfish, and self-absorbed. If you allow an evil spirit to rule you, "The acts of the sinful nature are obvious: sexual immorality, impurity, and debauchery, idolatry, and witchcraft; hatred, discord, jealousy, fits of rage, selfish ambition, dissensions, factions and envy, drunkenness, orgies, and the like." (Galatians 5:19-21 ESV) But, if you allow the Holy Spirit to lead you and guide you, His fruit will become more evident in your life. The fruit of the Holy Spirit are, "... love, joy, peace, patience, kindness, goodness, faithfulness, gentleness, and self-control." (Galatians 5:22-23 ESV) All of these wonderful things are produced in your life because of the Holy Spirit. Thank you, Holy Spirit.

You also receive spiritual gifts from the Holy Spirit. God gives each of us one or more spiritual gifts. Some gifts of the Holy Spirit are: words of knowledge, words of wisdom, gift of prophecy, gift of faith, gift of healing, working of miracles, discerning of spirits, speaking in tongues, and interpretation of tongues. (1 Corinthians 12:7-11) The gifts are given for the common good. God intends us each to grow and learn to use the gifts we have received within the church, or the body of Christ. When we all work together, displaying the fruit of the Spirit, and using the gifts of the Spirit, we become a powerful weapon for the Kingdom of God.

MERCENARIES

Some people are not motivated by allegiance, love, or truth, they just want to join the side that offers them the best reward and the most power. The spirit of mercenaries is greed and selfishness. That's just fine with Satan, he will tell you what you want to hear and sign you up to work for him. But, if you choose God, He checks your heart before accepting you in. Don't fool yourself, God knows the heart of every being and will judge us all accordingly, "People look at the outward appearance, but the Lord looks at the heart." (1 Samuel 16:7) Pretending to choose Christ, because He offers the most benefits will not end well.

Heed the story of Simon the Sorcerer. Simon saw the power, signs and miracles Peter and John were performing. Simon tried to pay them to receive this power, "Peter answered: 'May your money perish with you, because you thought you could buy the gift of God with money! You have no part or share in this ministry, because your heart is not right before God. Repent of this wickedness and pray to the Lord in the hope that he may forgive you for having such a thought in your heart. For I see you are full of bitterness and captive to sin." (Acts 8:20-23)

The God of all creation, the God who created you, will not be fooled and will not be mocked. He is surely powerful enough to search your heart and your intentions. King David wisely advised his son, "my son Solomon, acknowledge the God of your father, and serve him with wholehearted devotion and with a willing mind, for the Lord searches every heart and understands every desire and every thought. If you seek him, he will be found by you; but if you forsake him, he will reject you forever." (1 Chronicles 28:9)

CHOOSE JESUS TODAY

There is no time like the present. Today is a great day to be saved! Don't put off this decision for another day, "choose for yourselves this day whom you will serve." (Joshua 24:15) If you are still unsure, ask a simple question, "Jesus if you are real, would you reveal yourself to me?" God is faithful to reveal Himself to those who truly seek Him.

If you choose God, the Father, the Son, and the Holy Spirit, and are ready for a new life in Christ, the process is so simple a child can do it. There is no magical formula, amount of money, or works you need to do to get to heaven. The path to heaven is accepting and believing in Christ Jesus. He came to save the world. No matter who you are, He came, and He died to save you.

So, here it is, if you want to become a Christian, scripture tells us, "If you declare with your mouth, 'Jesus is Lord,' and believe in your heart that God raised him from the dead, you will be saved." (Romans 10:9) It's that simple. You can say out loud, **"Jesus you are Lord, and I believe God raised you from the dead. I want to be saved,"** and if you believe what you said, you are now saved!

But if you're ready to declare allegiance to Jesus, become a Christian, AND jump-start your relationship here is a more comprehensive prayer:

PRAY OUT LOUD

JESUS YOU ARE LORD! You are the Son of God, who died for my sins, and rose again on the third day. I surrender my life to you. Cleanse me God, remove every ounce of sin from me, and make me a new creation in you.

Your word says, if we confess our sins, you are faithful and just and will forgive us our sins and purify us from all unrighteousness. (1 John 1:9) Lord, I confess I am a sinner, and I ask you to cleanse me from all unrighteousness. God please show me the sins I need to confess.

(Take a moment to confess every sin God brings to your mind.)

Your word says, if we don't forgive others, you will not forgive our sins. (Matthew 6:15). Lord help me to forgive others, just as you have forgiven me. I don't want to hold anger, bitterness, pain, or wounds in my heart. God, please show me who I need to forgive.

(Take a moment to forgive everyone God brings to your mind.)

God please heal every wound in my mind, body, and soul. Make me whole, complete, and healthy.

Your word says you will baptize me with the Holy Spirit and fire. (Matthew 3:11) So, God I ask you to baptize me with the Holy Spirit and fire. I invite your Spirit to come dwell within me.

(Take a moment for God to release His Spirit on you.)

Thank you, God for loving me, for choosing me, for receiving me. God seal me and claim me as your own. I am now under your protection. I belong to you. I love you Lord.

Father help me fulfill every purpose and plan You have for my life and my calling. May every plan of the enemy against me fall to the ground and not prosper. God open my ears to hear Your voice and open my eyes to see what You show me. May You direct my path, and open doors to me, and may I remain on the path of righteousness all of the days of my life.

If you just spoke that prayer with a sincere heart, CONGRATULATIONS and WELCOME TO THE FAMILY! God is rejoicing! The angels are rejoicing! This is the best and most important decision you will ever make. It is a new time, a new season for your life. Please receive this blessing; speak it out loud over yourself.

> *I will continually ask God to fill me with the knowledge of His will through all the wisdom and understanding that the Spirit gives, so that I may live a life worthy of the Lord and please Him in every way; bearing fruit in every good work, growing in the knowledge of God, being strengthened with all power according to His glorious might so that I may have great endurance and patience, and giving joyful thanks to the Father, who has qualified me to share in the inheritance of His holy people in the kingdom of light. For He has rescued me from the dominion of darkness and brought me into the kingdom of the Son He loves, in whom I have redemption, the forgiveness of sins. - Colossians 1:9-14 personalized*

ALREADY A CHRISTIAN

Maybe you believe you are already a Christian, and maybe that's true. But the Bible tells us to, "…continue to work out your salvation with fear and trembling." (Philippians 2:12) Your salvation is too important to assume you are saved. Maybe you come from a Christian family. Maybe you have gone to church your whole life. Or, maybe you believe in Jesus. Satan believes Jesus is the Son of God. Satan knows scripture. But Satan is most assuredly not saved.

So how can you know if you are saved? How can you be sure you are in fact a Child of God? You must accept Christ as Lord of your life, as detailed in the previous section. It is very clear if God is Lord of your life, "This is how we know who the children of God are and who the children of the devil are: Anyone who does not do what is right is not God's child, nor is anyone who does not love their brother and sister." (1 John 3:10)

Love is an essential, "above all, love each other deeply, because love covers a multitude of sins." (1 Peter 4:8) It is also essential to turn from sin and follow God's commands. To continue to actively participate in a sinful lifestyle and claim that Jesus is Lord is contradictory. John wrote, "If we claim to have fellowship with him and yet walk in darkness, we lie and do not live out the truth." (1 John 1:6) To accept Christ does not mean that you will never sin again, but it does mean that we become increasingly aware of sin, and must continue to choose Christ over sin.

LUKEWARM

God warns, "I know your deeds, that you are neither cold nor hot. I wish you were either one or the other! So, because you are lukewarm – neither hot nor cold – I am about to spit you out of my mouth." (Revelation 3:15-16) There are no neutral territories or bench warmers in the spirit realm. There is no Switzerland, who can remain neutral and not choose a side in war. Jesus said, "Whoever is not with me is against me, and whoever does not gather with me scatters." (Matthew 12:30)

Imagine you're watching TV and you see the post-game interviews of your favorite team. An athlete said, "I believe in my team, I'm just not very actively involved." What?! Who wants that guy on the team? While watching another game you see a player who seems to wander from side to side. No one can tell what team he is on. It adds confusion to both teams and the entire scene. Then you flip the channel to another game and see that while the game is going, both teams are fiercely competing, but there aren't enough players on the field because their teammates are sitting on the bench, not interested, not prepared, or too afraid to join the game. The enemy tackles them anyway and continues to pummel them.

Can you continue in willful sin and be a Christian? The answer is no. The scripture is very clear here:

> *No one who lives in him keeps on sinning. No one who continues to sin has either seen him or known him. Dear children, do not let anyone lead you astray. The one who does what is right is righteous, just as he is righteous. The one who does what is sinful is of the devil, because the devil has been sinning from the beginning. The reason the Son of God appeared was to destroy the devil's work. No one who is born of God will continue to sin, because God's seed remains in them; they cannot go on sinning, because they have been born of God. This is how we know who the children of God are and who are the children of the devil are: Anyone who does not do what is right is not God's child, nor is anyone who does not love their brother or sister.*
> - *1 John 3:6-10*

So, herein lies your salvation's balancing act between your sin and God's mercy. God has the final say in each of our lives on Judgment Day. We don't know where the line is drawn and where each person will fall. But, the safe bet is to stay as far away from the line as possible. That means don't be lukewarm. Being half in and half out is not going to work. You're either all in with God or you're out.

Even so, in the spirit realm the enemy attacks everyone. Just because you haven't chosen a side, are lukewarm, remained undecided, or uncommitted, doesn't mean that you aren't on the battlefield and open to attack. We are all in this battle, whether we like it or not, or realize it or not.

"WHO DO YOU RUN TO"

We must all choose our master and where our allegiance lies. It is true that, "No one can serve two masters. Either you will hate the one and love the other, or you will be devoted to the one and despise the other. You cannot serve both God and money." (Matthew 6:24) You can replace the word "money" with anything else. You cannot serve God and any other master. Even good things can become an idol if we serve them and are devoted to them more than God. The first commandment is, "You shall have no other gods before me." (Exodus 20:3)

Over and over we see God chastising the Israelites for choosing other gods before him. And He reminded them over and over, "I am the Lord your God." (Judges 6:10) They looked to form alliances with other nations, to secure peace. God told them to look to Him, to seek Him, to ask Him for everything they need. The circumstances may be different, but those same concepts apply to us as individuals. Take a moment to examine your life. Who or what you serve reveals where your allegiance lies. The lyrics of the song, "Who do you run to?" ask some good questions:

> You got 24 hours to serve and pray to your god.
> Who do you run to?
> Where you put your money and you put your mind,
> Where you give your love and you give your time, is your god.
> Who do you run to?
> Do I long for time with you each day? Do I listen to the words you say?
>
> Day by day as the trials come
> You get to choose where your help comes from, what god?
> Who do you run to?
> From the world around you options rise,
> You will likely choose where you set your eyes upon.
> Who do you run to?
> Do I look to you to save the day? Do I look to you to make a way?

... choose for yourselves this day whom you will serve, whether the gods of your ancestors served beyond the Euphrates, or the gods of the Amorites, in whose land you are living. But as for me and my household, we will serve the Lord.
- Joshua 24:15

The journey into the rest of this book starts here. You must choose your master and declare allegiance to God the Father, the Son Jesus, and the Holy Spirit, or there is no Core connection. There is no way to Prepare for life's battles and judgment day without Christ. Everything starts here.

Take all the time you need to make this decision.
But, do not put it off until later. It is too important.

If you chose to declare allegiance to God; the Father, the Son Jesus, and the Holy Spirit, congratulations! You are now ready to become a Prepared Warrior.

But thanks be to God that, though you used to be slaves to sin, you have come to obey from your heart the pattern of teaching that has now claimed your allegiance. - Romans 6:17 (underline added)

PART 2

PREPARED WARRIORS

Chapter 5

TJ'S STORY
BATTLEGROUND

TJ hit the ground running. He could feel the energy coursing through his body. There was a new awakening in his spirit that was just electrifying. He couldn't quite explain it except to say that he felt so much lighter, and so free, like a bird flying high in the sky. He wanted to tell everyone about Jesus. TJ just knew they would be as excited as he was, if they only knew the truth about Jesus.

First TJ started off by telling his mom all about his experience. He wanted her to know Jesus too! Jesus could help her so much with all the stress she had in her life. She was excited for TJ and could tell something different had definitely happened. But she had a look on her face that said, "let me wait and see how this plays out." That's OK. TJ knew this was real and would stand the test of time.

Next, TJ started sharing Jesus with people at school. Some people were already Christians and welcomed him to the family. Others looked at him like he was crazy and walked the other way quickly. TJ knew he needed to refine his approach, but it was so hard to stop talking about Jesus now that he finally found something real.

As TJ went about his day the demons peered around the corner, watching from a distance. This new convert threw off their daily rounds. They had to recalculate and reassess their missions. There would have to be new attacks, new defenses set up, and more demons brought in to contain the fire.

In the spirit realm TJ was now on fire. The Holy Spirit showed around him like a bright fire, burning and alive with the Spirit. The demons knew better than to approach him in this condition. The fire would instantly consume them. They had to bide their time, waiting and plotting their next move.

In addition to the fire, a new angel, Nigel, had arrived. Nigel was glorious and bright. He stood at attention and stayed right beside TJ as he moved throughout his day. The angel was always alert and aware of the demons' positions, even when they did their best to hide. Nigel's size wasn't as menacing as the fierce look in his eyes. The demons knew better than to challenge him directly. They would have to be smart.

TJ started attending church with Teyo. Teyo really had a great church family. The Pastor taught the Bible and made it so clear TJ could even understand it. There really are a lot of interesting stories in there. TJ had no idea how honest the Bible was, even showing people's faults and sins. But there were always opportunities for them to turn back to God. That gave TJ such great relief. He learned he didn't have to be perfect, just keep turning back to God.

TJ also discovered he loved to worship. Songs started to come alive to him now. The lyrics started to make sense and he could feel God's warm presence as he sang. TJ was still new to the whole praying thing, and he didn't quite understand it. But that would come.

TJ was now becoming known at school as a Christian. He didn't mind people knowing, in fact he still talked openly about his faith, new exciting things he was learning, and sharing Jesus with anyone who would listen.

But then, some of the kids started hurling insults at him. They started calling him, "weird," "cult leader," and "Bible beater." Other kids thought it was funny and started joining in. It wasn't funny to TJ, and he knew those things weren't true, but it was hard to dodge them when they came around, and TJ wasn't sure how to respond.

There was a great cheer of victory from the group of demons gathered together to watch their plan play out. They had worked for weeks laying the groundwork for this mission. They brought in the experts Slander, Gossip, and Insult. The demons worked together to whisper slander in the ears of the kids at school. They made a point to attack anyone within earshot of TJ sharing Jesus with someone. They followed TJ at a comfortable distance. Then, as soon as TJ stopped to talk, they jumped on the back of someone near, and started going to work, "Can you believe that kid? All he does is talk about Jesus! What makes him think anyone cares? No one likes him. See how annoyed they are? Make sure he sees you glaring at him, so he won't come talk to you. Who does he think he is? Bible beater! Cult leader! Weirdo!" Yes, this plan was working perfectly. It only took about a week for the demons' whispers to become words out of the kids' mouths. They were so easy to manipulate! So easy to control. The demons didn't have to go anywhere near the Holy Spirit-filled TJ, they just let the kids do the work for them.

The demons held such hate-filled satisfaction every time one of their kids spoke the exact words they whispered. In the spirit realm, the demons could see that the words actually held more power than the kids realized. Each time someone said, "No one likes you! Stop talking weirdo!" The demons could see an arrow shoot from the kid's mouth straight to TJ's heart. A shout of victory would go up from all the surrounding demons. The demons know the Word of God says, "the power of life and death is in the tongue," they plan to use the venomous arrows over and over until their enemy falls. (Proverbs 18:21)

TJ knew enough to know he shouldn't let their words hurt him. But he felt a sting of pain every time someone insulted him, and others laughed. He would move on, but later, as he tried to sleep, their words would replay in his head. Over and over he would hear them. They weren't right. They were mean. But TJ wasn't sure how to respond now that he is a Christian. Once he heard someone say, "What would Jesus do?" That's exactly what TJ planned to figure out!

Chapter 6

PREPARED WARRIORS

When you chose Jesus, you became a part of His Kingdom, or His team. Congratulations, you chose the winning team! The kingdom of God is filled with the people from the vast variety of His creation. There is no one type of person that is called to be a part of God's Kingdom. It's not just for the super religious, or the beginner Christian, or for people who are active in the ministry. Every person in the Kingdom is important to the team. Every person has a role and jobs which God has given you to complete. God intends each person to grow and learn and accomplish all He created you to do. God's says, "For I know the plans I have for you,' declares the Lord, 'plans to prosper you and not to harm you, plans to give you hope and a future.'" (Jeremiah 29:11) But, the devil, "comes only to steal and kill and destroy." (John 10:10)

For that reason, every person in the Kingdom of God must prepare for battle. If you choose not to prepare, life will not stop coming at you, and the enemy will not stop attacking you. You become an easy target of the enemy if you are not prepared and stand with no weapons or armor. But if you choose to Prepare, you will have weapons to counter the enemy's attack, and your armor will protect you. It is not difficult, super time consuming, or too hard to become a warrior. Consistently taking simple steps you can become a Prepared Warrior. So, this book is for you, no matter who you are, or what is going on in your life. It is for all who seek God and want to live in victory here on earth.

YOUNG WARRIORS

Young Warriors will rise. They have faced temptation, endured mean and unkind peers, struggles within their homes, and within their own minds. They realize that the enemy has no regard for their age. The enemy intends to destroy them, but Young Warriors will not go down easily. There are those who will endure, and seek, and find that there can be victory even in the midst of their struggle. They will find they are not alone. They will never be alone. They will grow stronger as they survive every attack. They will learn to recognize the enemy controlling the people. They will learn that the enemy lies even in their own minds. They will learn to wait and listen for the Savior's still small voice. They will find peace. They will carry it with them. Now, Young Warriors begin to Prepare for life's battles and judgment day.

NEW WARRIORS

New Warriors will join the fight. They had their eyes open to the way, the truth, and the life. Now that they have seen the truth, they come to the fight with a new purpose. There is much to learn, and the time is short. The enemy will not give them up without a fight. The attacks swirl around them. The enemy plans to take them down before they are firmly planted and connected to the Core. But the more they learn, the firmer their stance becomes. They are drawn to the Core because nowhere else have they found such pure relentless love, acceptance, and peace. Now, New Warriors begin to Prepare for life's battles and judgment day.

SLEEPING WARRIORS

Sleeping Warriors begin to wake. They may have believed in God their whole lives, but never realized the pressing need to connect to the Core. They knew of God but did not "know" God. They thought of God as a piece of their lives, amidst their busy schedule, that need not get in the way of their own personal pursuits. But even as they moved, day by day, the enemy set up traps, and snares, and cornered them, thirsting to destroy them. They were not even aware the enemy was behind it all. But as the enemy brought them to their knees, he did not expect them to call on the name of Jesus. The enemy did not imagine that the more he attacked them, the attacks the sleeping warriors would eventually awaken. Now they are aware of the enemy's existence, and plans to kill, steal, and destroy them and their families. Now they know. Now they are awake and aware. Now, Awake Warriors begin to Prepare for life's battles and judgment day.

SEASONED WARRIORS

Seasoned Warriors have not given up. They have learned the truth of God, they have endured many trials, and assaults from the enemy. They have earned their stripes. But even as the years pass, the battle wages on, the new and young warriors show up with vigor, and the new generation of prophecy teachers declare the time of the end is near. The warrior's zest for preparing has dwindled, their certainty of Christ's return has waned, and they are biding their time until they retire into God's kingdom. But the horizon reveals new threats. The coming days are likely to contain struggles, battles, and persecution. However, they will not be caught complacent and unaware. Seasoned Warriors won't tap out just yet. They aim to finish the race and complete the task the Lord Jesus has given them. (Acts 20:24) The seasoned warriors fill their lamp with oil while they can. (Matthew 25:1-13) They daily renew their connection to the Core and join with the new and young warriors to share their wisdom and encourage them. Every warrior is needed in this hour. Now, Seasoned Warriors once again Prepare for life's battles and judgment day.

REMNANT WARRIORS

Remnant Warriors are created "for such a time as this." (Esther 4:14) These warriors understand the hour we live in. They know it is important to, "Put on the full armor of God so that you can take a stand against the devil's schemes… so that when the day of evil comes, you may be able to stand your ground…" (Ephesians 6:11, 13) They love and serve the Lord Jesus with all of their heart. They regularly connect to the Core. God refreshes them and directs them daily. They embrace the Holy Spirit, direction, correction, and guidance. There is no other god or idol to distract their focus. They keep a short account with God, regularly repenting and forgiving. They are about the Father's business. They are thirsty for new wisdom and understanding from God about Him and His kingdom. Their goal is to be as prepared as they can be for spiritual battles on earth, and for the White throne judgment in Heaven. Now, Remnant Warriors continue to Prepare for life's battles and judgment day.

Each Warrior plays a role in the Kingdom of God. You are important. You are important to God, to your family, friends, co-workers, classmates, and to the many people you can help, love, care for, and bless. Your life is bigger than you can imagine. Your impact is greater than you can imagine. God has perfect sight. He knows the end from the beginning. He knows exactly why He created you, and all He intends for you to accomplish. Let God take over and direct you. When He guides you, the reach of your smallest deeds can have amazing eternal impact and blessings. You can be a game changer for your family, friends, classmates, co-workers, and those you serve. One willing Warrior can start a fire that others see and respond to. The more Warriors in the house, the less the enemy wants to enter! Just one Warrior can chase a thousand enemies, but two put ten thousand to flight! (Deuteronomy 32:30)

Though this book is focused on our individual connection to the Core, it is not an endorsement for isolated spiritual existence. Our success in battle is much more likely when we work together. We were never intended to be alone, "The Lord God said, 'It is not good for the man to be alone. I will make a helper suitable for him.'" (Genesis 2:18)

We are a team, a unit, of diverse people, experiences, backgrounds, and parts of our spiritual journeys. The enemy plans to divide and conquer us. But when we all commit to become Prepared Warriors, connecting to the

Core, we can more easily work together, helping one another, joining forces to be victorious. It is true, "Though one may be overpowered, two can defend themselves. A cord of three strands is not quickly broken." (Ecclesiastes 4:12)

Like many topics in this book, the unity of believers is a concept worthy of its own book. But the first step toward working together and moving in the same direction is individually connecting to the Core. If we all seek God regularly, receiving His correction and direction, and surrender our own agendas, we have a great start at unity.

The enemy's strategy of divide and conquer, is counter to what God wants. The Apostle Paul shares God's plan, "I appeal to you, brothers and sisters, in the name of our Lord Jesus Christ, that all of you agree with one another in what you say and that there be no division among you, but that you be perfectly united in mind and thought." (1 Corinthians 1:10) God calls us to perfect unity in mind and thought through Him.

We accomplish perfect unity by all being connected to the Core. In a glimpse of heavenly praise, we hear those around the throne of God sing, "... and with your blood you purchased for God persons from every tribe and language and people and nation. You have made them to be a kingdom and priests to serve our God, and they will reign on the earth." (Rev 5:9-10) God has called people from every tribe, language and nation to be a part of His Kingdom, to be His people, His Warriors.

The Apostle John, in his letter, called out the Warriors of every age, "I am writing to you, dear children, because your sins have been forgiven on account of his name. I am writing to you, fathers, because you know him who is from the beginning. I am writing to you, young men, because you have overcome the evil one. I write to you dear children, because you know the Father. I write to you, fathers, because you know him who is from the beginning. I write to you, young men, because you are strong, and the word of God lives in you, and you have overcome the evil one." (1 John 2:12-14) Likewise, we are calling Warriors of all ages to arise!

Chapter 7

PREPARED FOR VICTORY

*...for everyone born of God overcomes the world. This is the victory that has
overcome the world, even our faith. Who is it that overcomes the world?
Only the one who believes that Jesus is the Son of God.*
1 John 5:4-5

Our first goal is to help warriors prepare for victory. Being prepared for victory, is winning the battle in your mind over who you will believe. Do you believe God or the enemy? It is easy to say you believe God, but when the battle comes are you overcome with worry? Worry is the opposite of faith. Faith believes God. Fear, worry, and anxiety happen when you doubt and listen to the devil.

The devil is the father of lies (John 8:44). He will have you defeated before you even get out of bed in the morning. His words in your mind tear you down, discourage you, depress you, and stop you from believing God. ATTENTION!! These are not your thoughts, they are the devil's persistent attacks, and you have started to agree with him! Do not agree with him. Stop listening to him! He is a liar! You can counter every lie with the truth found in scripture. If he says, "Nobody loves you." Speak out loud, "I am God's chosen person, holy and dearly loved." (personalized Colossians 3:12) The Bible tells us if we resist the devil he will flee. (James 4:7) It's true. If Jesus used scripture to counter and resist the devil, then we should too. (Matthew 4:1-11)

Faith is a key component in determining what we believe. We see the sun rise every morning, so we have faith and believe it will occur again tomorrow. If you haven't seen the sun rise ever before, it would be much harder to have faith that it would happen, causing you to believe it may not happen. If you don't believe it's even possible, you won't "believe" God can do it. But, if you believe God can do anything, you have faith He will do it. Do you have enough faith to believe God can help you? Here is some good news, Jesus said, "Truly I tell you, if you have faith as small as a mustard seed, you can say to this mountain, 'Move from here to there,' and it will move. Nothing will be impossible for you." (Matthew 17:20) You don't have to have the greatest, most amazing faith to have victory. Jesus said if you even have faith as small as a mustard seed you can have great victory! Once you see God move in a small victory, it's easier to believe He will move the next time you need a victory. That's how your faith grows, until you are finally believing Him for the impossible, huge things! Faith is essential for victory.

Believing God is able, and believing God is willing are two different things. You may agree that God is able to do amazing things but believing God will do that for you may be a harder pill to swallow. Ultimately, the knowledge of God's greatness is much easier to accept, than His great love and care for us.

We hear about God healing people, but believing, really believing God will heal you is much harder. We hear that God answered the prayers of a mother and father who desperately prayed for a lost son or daughter, who miraculously accepts Christ. But, it's much harder to believe God could actually save your son or daughter, who has rejected every attempt you have made to share the gospel. Is God able to do these things for you? Is God willing to do these things for you? The answer is YES, "The LORD is my strength and my shield; my heart trusts in him, and he helps me." (Psalm 28:7a)

The better you know God, the more your faith in Him will grow. No matter what your circumstances are, you will know that God will take care of you. God is faithful. God is loving and kind. God is full of mercy and grace. God is all powerful. God is your protector and provider. Do you know God well enough to be content no matter what your circumstances? (Phil 4:12) When you get to that point, the battle may still be waging on, your circumstances may still be the same, but you are not.

The whole atmosphere around you shifts once you begin to believe God can and will move in your life. When you connect with the Core, and believe God's great power and love for you, that's when you know you are Prepared for Victory.

VICTORY

It is your inheritance as a child of God, to live in victory, "for everyone born of God overcomes the world. This is the victory that has overcome the world, even our faith. Who is it that overcomes the world? Only the one who believes that Jesus is the Son of God." (1 John 5:4-5) Believing Jesus gives you victory. When you start from a place of victory, it is harder to pull you down. The prince, the son of the most powerful King, doesn't possess a lowly demeanor of fear or defeat. No, the prince presents himself in a confident, courageous manner, as one who assumes victory over his foes.

His confidence lies in the belief that his father, the King, and his kingdom are secure. Likewise, as children of the King, our confidence and courage come from our Father, who is the King above all Kings, and whose kingdom is unshakeable. So, stand strong, "You, dear children, are from God and have overcome them, because the one who is in you is greater than the one who is in the world." (1 John 4:4) God is greater than any enemy you will ever face, "If God is for us, who can be against us?" (Romans 8:31)

Who can defeat God? The devil already tried and failed; he was cast out of heaven. God's victory is assured because He is more powerful than Satan. The Bible says that Christians will also triumph over Satan, "They triumphed over him by the blood of the Lamb and by the word of their testimony; they did not love their lives so much as to shrink from death." (Revelation 12:10-11) They stood with Christ, even if it cost them their lives. That is victory! Did you note the weapon and armor in the scripture? The Christian's armor is the protective covering of the "blood of the lamb," which is accepting Christ's blood as a payment for our sins. The weapon is the "the word of their testimony," which is speaking of the wonderful things God has done. The Christian's victory is assured because our weapons and armor are more powerful than Satan.

The Lord is always victorious! He never loses. Even when the devil thinks he wins, he doesn't! Like when Christ was crucified on the cross, which actually ends up purchasing redemption for all mankind's sins! You can call that a HUGE victory! Hello! God outsmarts the devil every time. He knows the beginning and the end of your story. He can work every battle, struggle, mistake, or sin for His good, and your good (Rom 8:28). He is the amazing miracle worker, who takes dust and turns it into us! What can't He do? Need more convincing? Read your Bible! It is filled with stories of how God fights for His people. How He uses the unlikely. How He wins against unbelievable odds, in fact He likes it that way!

Then, one final victory over Satan is prophesied to happen. The prophecy is at the end of the Bible in the book of Revelations, "And the devil, who deceived them, was thrown into the lake of burning sulfur, where the beast and the false prophet had been thrown. They will be tormented day and night for ever and ever." (Revelation 20:10) God wins every time. We must take the important step of knowing the scriptures, to believing the scriptures. Then, we must believe that as a child of God, His victory extends to us. "Those who are victorious will inherit all this, and I will be their God and they will be my children." (Revelation 21:7) Victory is our inheritance!

GOD IS A WARRIOR

The LORD will go forth like a warrior, He will arouse His zeal like a man of war. He will utter a shout, yes, He will raise a war cry. He will prevail against His enemies.
- Isaiah 42:13

Like a chess master, who knows the end of the game before it begins, we can be assured victory because we know our opponent's moves, and we know how to counter every one of them. Most importantly, and this is not cheating, God, who knows the beginning and the end, is there to whisper in your ear every move before you make it.

Imagine having the fiercest warrior of all time there to lead you into battle, and actually fight it for you. That is exactly what you have, "For the Lord you God is the one who goes with you to fight for you against your enemies to give you victory." (Deuteronomy 20:4) Did you know that? It's true, "The Lord is a warrior; the Lord is his name." (Exodus 15:3)

Maybe you didn't know that about God. It's common for people to focus on one attribute of God, like love, and dismiss all the other parts of who He is. But, if you read the word of God, you will see God is multifaceted and complex, and powerful. The prophet Isaiah declared, "The Lord will march out like a champion, like a warrior he will stir up his zeal; with a shout he will raise the battle cry and will triumph over his enemies." (Isaiah 42:13)

The Lord is a fierce warrior, he is a champion, and we are made in His image! (Genesis 1:26) We are made to be like Him, we are made to be with Him. God loves you. He doesn't want to see you defeated. Timothy knew, "The Lord will rescue me from every evil attack and will bring me safely to his heavenly kingdom. To him be glory for ever and ever. Amen." (2 Timothy 4:18)

Yes, battles will come. But you don't have to fight them by yourself. You are not alone. Over and over in scripture we see, "the Lord will fight for you." (Deuteronomy 1:30, Deuteronomy 3:22, Ex 14:14, Nehemiah 4:20… etc.) God does not expect us to fight the devil on our own. He is ready and willing to fight for us!

> **But be assured today that the Lord your God is the one who goes across ahead of you like a devouring fire. _He will destroy them_; he will subdue them before you. And you will drive them out and annihilate them quickly, as the Lord has promised you.**
> **- Deuteronomy 9:3 underline added**

God gives victory to his people through various different methods. In the Bible you will find many examples of the Israelites winning without even fighting their enemy. Just believing and obeying God was enough to win the battle. In the amazing story of the Israelites' exodus out of Egypt, God told Moses exactly what to do. But when the enemy surrounded them, the Israelites were afraid. Moses told the people, "Do not be afraid. Stand firm and you will see the deliverance the Lord will bring you today. The Egyptians you see today you will never see again. The Lord will fight for you; you need only be still." (Exodus 14:14) Now imagine hearing those words and trying to believe them.

The Egyptians were their slave masters for hundreds of years. They were warriors on horses, surrounding the Israelites, who were without weapons of any kind. The Israelites struggled to believe and obey what God said. So, "Then the Lord said to Moses, 'Why are you crying out to me? Tell the Israelites to move on.'" (Exodus 14:15) Keep moving! Believe and obey!

Believing and obeying God is often the hardest battle we fight. Once we believe and obey God, He fights the battle for us, "For the Lord your God is the one who goes with you to fight for you against your enemies to give you victory." (Deuteronomy 20:4) God fights for us and gives us victory every time we believe and obey.

So, here you are today, surrounded by the enemy, struggling to hear God and obey. But you are willing to fight and ask God for victory. Your battle is not a surprise to God. Jesus told us, "In this world you will have trouble. But take heart! I have overcome the world." (John 16:33) Jesus showed us the way, He is our best example. Jesus was victorious right? He overcame death and the grave. But, remember, not every moment of his life looked like victory in the moment. Victory in heaven doesn't always look like victory on earth. Like a well-crafted story, our lives play out in a series of hills and valleys, trials and triumphs. You cannot judge your full story based on today's trials.

In most battles, your own personal strength determines if you win. But your victory is not determined by your strength. In spiritual battle, your victory is tied to your allegiance and what master you choose. When you chose Jesus, you chose victory. It is God's strength that wins your battles, "I can do all things through him who gives me strength." (Philippians 4:13) God's strength is a shield for believers, "Through you we push back our enemies; through your name we trample our foes." (Psalm 44:5) Just the name of Jesus is powerful enough to trample our foes!

Also, as God's child, He gives you authority over demons, "I have given you authority to trample on snakes and scorpions and to overcome all the power of the enemy; nothing will harm you." (Luke 10:19) Realizing the authority and victory we have as children of God is crucial for standing in victory. You are not defenseless. You are not a victim to the attacks of the enemy. You are well equipped and able to overcome and be victorious.

God said, through His prophet Isaiah, "'No weapon forged against you will prevail, and you will refute every tongue that accuses you. This is the heritage of the servants of the Lord, and this is their vindication from me' declares the Lord." (Isaiah 54:17) The enemy has no weapon that can overtake you. There is nothing more powerful than the Lord, the ultimate warrior. Nothing stands up to God, but all things fall to Him.

ENEMY ATTACKS BUT DOES NOT WIN

From the beginning of our human existence, with Adam and Eve, the devil has been trying to draw people away from God, then he attacks. Those in the early church were well aware of the devil's tactics, "Therefore, dear friends, since you have been forewarned, be on your guard so that you may not be carried away by the error of the lawless and fall from your secure position. But grow in the grace and knowledge of our Lord and Savior Jesus Christ. To him be glory both now and forever! Amen." (2 Peter 3:17-18) Yes, battles will come, but drawing close to God is always the right answer. It is exactly opposite of what the devil hopes to accomplish with his assaults.

The enemy hopes to catch us unaware, and unprepared for battle. But as we commit to become Prepared Warriors, we become harder to conquer. The apostle Peter said, "Dear friends, do not be surprised at the fiery ordeal that has come on you to test you, as though something strange were happening to you." (1 Peter 4:12) It is not strange; it is not a surprise that the devil attacks us. He made his position very clear.

Be ready, "Be alert and of sober mind. Your enemy the devil prowls around like a roaring lion looking for someone to devour. Resist him, standing firm in the faith, because you know that the family of believers throughout the world is undergoing the same kind of sufferings." (1 Peter 5:8-9) It's true the enemy is looking for someone to devour. Yes, the enemy will attack, but he will not win!

God is our strength, our refuge, and our renewal, "but those who hope in the LORD will renew their strength. They will soar on wings like eagles; they will run and not grow weary, they will walk and not be faint." (Isaiah 40:31) Our connection to God, the Core, is essential for victory. The closer you are to God, the less the enemy wants to fight you. Like a bully on the playground, if you stand next to the teacher, he will leave you alone. It is the same in the spiritual world. Stand next to God, never leave His side, let Him defend you, and keep the enemy at bay.

Chapter 8

PREPARE FOR LIFE'S BATTLES

Our next goal is to help warriors prepare for life's battles. Preparing for battle takes daily training. Showing up is not enough. You can show up to a marathon, but you will most likely not make it to the finish line if you haven't trained and prepared for the race. There is no off-season for spiritual warfare. Like any true warrior, it is wise to get ready and stay ready. The first and most important step for training and preparing for war is to connect to the Core before you go to war.

This book will provide you with detailed directions for how to connect. Learning about God through books, videos, sermons and other sources is important. But it cannot replace the Core connection. That is where your actual training and preparing takes place. Connecting to God, learning about God from God is irreplaceable and of utmost importance!

What if you were in the presence of the King, but instead of speaking to him you read in a book about him, watch a video about him, or listen to a teacher talk about him. But, he's in the room! Speak to him! Listen to him! Learn from him! You have direct contact with the King of Kings! Why go to another source?

Training and preparing with Core connection helps you gain a secure position. In "The Art of War" by Sun Tzu, he teaches, "the skillful fighter puts himself into a position which makes defeat impossible, and does not miss the moment for defeating the enemy." Gain your secure position first; for Christians our secure position is beneath the wing of the Almighty.

The Psalmist writes, "If you say, 'The Lord is my refuge,' and you make the Most High your dwelling, no harm will overtake you, no disaster will come near your tent. For he will command his angels concerning you to guard you in all your ways; they will lift you up in their hands, so that you will not strike your foot against a stone. You will tread on the lion and the cobra; you will trample the great lion and the serpent." (Psalm 91:9-13) When we position ourselves as close as possible to God, it makes our defeat impossible.

Once you are trained and prepared, you just have to be on your guard, watching for enemy attack, "Therefore, dear friends, since you have been forewarned, be on your guard so that you may not be carried away by the error of the lawless and fall from your secure position. But grow in the grace and knowledge of our Lord and Savior Jesus Christ. To him be glory both now and forever! Amen." (2 Peter 3:17-18) Peter encourages the believers to continue to "grow in the grace and knowledge of our Lord and Savior." Spiritual training and preparation are as simple as learning about and becoming more like the Savior. We call Him Master because He is our great and respected teacher. Our job is to become more like the Master, our teacher, "… but everyone who is fully trained will be like their teacher." (Luke 6:40) If you remember that simple instruction, you can train and prepare with laser focus.

LIFE'S BATTLES

Every person has his or her own life experience, and spiritual journey, but we all have one thing in common, battles. Battles come in all shapes and sizes and are as constant and universal as the air we breathe. Some people's battles are obvious or known, while other people appear to have it all together without a care in the world. The truth is that everyone has battles, some people are just better at hiding it; some are just better at fighting it! How we see these battles, how we respond in battle, and how we emerge after a battle is of great importance.

Battles reveal and shape our character. They teach us lessons and help us gain wisdom. They help prepare us for the next battle. There is always a next battle. The question is, "Are you Prepared?" The wisdom of Sun Tzu explains, "The art of war teaches us to rely not on the likelihood of the enemy's not coming, but on our own readiness to receive him; not on the chance of his not attacking, but rather on the fact that we have made our position unassailable." ("The Art of War" by Sun Tzu) The battle will surely come, and preparation is essential to victory.

Jesus warned his disciples of battles, "I am sending you out like sheep among wolves. Therefore, be as shrewd as snakes and as innocent as doves." (Matthew 10:16) Was he sending his disciples into war? No, he was sending them out to share the good news of the Kingdom of God! But He knew that they were taking light into dark places. The enemy will always fight back against what God is doing.

Peter advised the early Christians, "Dear friends, do not be surprised at the fiery ordeal that has come on you to test you, as though something strange were happening to you." (1 Peter 4:16) It really should be no surprise that hard times, challenges, and difficulties are part of life. As Christians we are told to expect it. We should expect the enemy to attack us, we should expect to be persecuted as Jesus was persecuted, and should we expect God will test our faith, as He tested Abraham, and so many others in the Bible. We see it all around us; yet, when it happens to us, we are somehow surprised, and often unprepared. Let's change that.

What battles are you fighting? Some battles are obvious and easy to spot. You know you are being attacked and feel the weight of each blow the enemy throws. Other battles are more subtle and harder to discern. There are three categories of battle: Internal, External, and Territorial.

Internal battles happen within your mind and spirit. The internal battles are against your own sinful nature, or current mental state, and often a demonic presence. For instance, you may be depressed due to circumstances in your life, or a chemical imbalance. But, then the spirit of depression comes and adds extra weight and pull to draw you further down. The demonic spirit often presents itself as a comfortable friend, enticing you to stay in that state, or keep coming back to it. But it ultimately leads to death.

Another example is anger. You may be at a sporting event and get angry at a call from the referee. But, the spirit of anger draws you into anger at a level you no longer feel in control of yourself. You continue to yell, and it takes you hours to calm down. Internal battles involve demons on covert missions, much like a spy. They implant themselves in your mind, as a friendly companion, flying below radar, so you barely notice their whispers or the control they gradually gain over you.

Internal spiritual battles are more difficult to discern and often take the Holy Spirit or wise discerning Christian to point them out. You may have had the issue your whole life and accepted it as normal. When in fact, there has been a generational demonic stronghold over you and your family in that area. Some families collectively have the same struggle, which has become a generational curse. An entire family may battle gluttony, feeding into each other's struggle. A mother may battle the spirit of fear and pass on her own fear to her children. Now they all live in fear together, accepting it as normal. Fear should not be accepted as normal, "For God did not give us a spirit of fear. He gave us a spirit of power and of love and of a good mind." (2 Timothy 1:7 NLV) There are many internal battles that can occur; here is a short list to consider:

INTERNAL BATTLES

Fear	Selfishness	Gluttony
Depression	Pride	Sexual Perversion
Anxiety	Lust	Hopelessness
Anger & Bitterness	Greed	Insecurity
Loneliness	Deception	Laziness
Negativity	Jealousy	Judgmental
Control	Worthlessness	
Manipulate	Self-Pity	

The first step to victory over internal battles is establishing and maintaining a Core connection.

External spiritual battles affect you personally or those closest to you. They can affect your body, your relationships, your finances, etc. For example, maybe you suffer from ongoing health problems. Or maybe your family continues to struggle with finances year after year. Maybe you or someone you love struggles with addiction, pulling you through the same terrible cycle of dependency. External battles hit hard and can be long term battles.

However, external battles are the easiest to discern. There is no covert demonic coddling, and enticement here. They present themselves in the physical realm, so we clearly see when we are under attack. External spiritual battles are more like the Air Force, dropping bombs on you and those you love. But they can also be the hardest to endure. External battles can overwhelm us and make everyday life so difficult. Most people have at least one area of their life that is under attack by the enemy. But when the enemy is really trying to destroy you, he will drop bombs in several areas at the same time. There are many external battles that can occur; here is a short list to consider:

EXTERNAL BATTLES

Relationship Problems
Abuse
Addictions
Health Problems

Financial Problems
Career Problems
Premature or Sudden Deaths

The first step to victory over external battles is establishing and maintaining a Core connection.

Territorial spiritual battles occur whenever a child of God enters enemy territory. Though Christians, because we have the Holy Spirit, have spiritual authority wherever we go, most do not realize they carry this authority, and do not use it. The enemy has no regard for your authority if you don't use it. If you don't take charge of the spiritual atmosphere, the enemy is glad to take the lead. Can you imagine soldiers entering enemy territory and then just sitting down to hang out? The enemy would swarm them, overtake them, and destroy them within minutes. It is the same thing in the spiritual realm.

But what is enemy territory? Essentially the whole earth is enemy territory, until a Christian moves in and takes authority. Your home, your school, your work, your city, your state, your country, even your church may be enemy territory. But all of those locations are actually YOUR territory, under your authority, through the Holy Spirit. Each Christian is responsible for claiming and defending their own territory. Prepared Warriors mission is to prepare you to protect and defend you, your household and your territory.

When you take authority over the evil spirits in your territory, there may still be a battle for control. Some demons realize they are defeated from the beginning, but others may be unwilling to surrender, and take greater spiritual weapons to defeat. Some demons are attached to the territory, and others are attached to the people in the territory. But either way your weapons of warfare are the same: Word, Worship and Prayer. There are many Territorial Battles; here is a short list to consider:

TERRITORIAL

Home
School
Work
Specific location

City
State
Country

The first step to victory over territorial battles is establishing and maintaining a Core connection.

GREAT TRIBULATION & THE ANTI-CHRIST

There is one final battle at the end of this age, known in the Bible as the Great Tribulation. In this period of time Jesus describes a great battle for believers, "Then you will be handed over to be persecuted and put to death, and you will be hated by all nations because of me. At that time many will turn away from the faith and will betray and hate each other, and many false prophets will appear and deceive many people. Because of the increase of wickedness, the love of most will grow cold." (Matthew 24:9-12) This period of time is described to be a very difficult time for Christians and all people.

It is possible we could witness the Great Tribulation. The Bible gives us a clear understanding of what to expect, so we can recognize if we are in that time and prepare to stand with God, and resist the devil. During this period of time the anti-Christ, the beast, will rise into power to become the ruler over the whole world. He will force, "...all people, great and small, rich and poor, free and slave, to receive a mark on their right hands or on their foreheads, so that they could not buy or sell unless they had the mark, which is the name of the beast or the number of its name. (Revelation 13:15-17) The mark of the beast being required will be a clear sign that you must heed and resist, even if it means your death.

Prepare now. Decide that NEVER, under any circumstances, will you or your family take the mark of the beast. You must trust and remain faithful to God, even unto death.

Why is it so important that you not take the mark of the beast? The Bible says this about those who take the mark of the beast, "If anyone worships the beast and its image and receives its mark on their forehead or on their hand, they, too, will drink the wine of God's fury, which has been poured full strength into the cup of his wrath. They will be tormented with burning sulfur in the presence of the holy angels and of the Lamb. And the smoke of their torment will rise for ever and ever. There will be no rest day or night for those who worship the beast and its image, or for anyone who receives the mark of its name." (Revelation 14:9-11)

But, if you are prepared, you do not take the mark, and stand with God, the Bible says, "And I saw the souls of those who had been beheaded because of their testimony about Jesus and because of the word of God. They had not worshiped the beast or its image and had not received its mark on their foreheads or their hands. They came to life and reigned with Christ a thousand years." (Revelation 20:4) Those who stand firm to the end will come to life and reign with Christ. You will receive eternal rewards for your temporary suffering.

We may be the generation that is destined to endure through the Great Tribulation. But, even if we are not, there is currently unprecedented Christian persecution all over the world. We must prepare to endure persecution and even death without denouncing our faith in Jesus Christ. Jesus continued to say, "but the one who stands firm to the end will be saved." (Matthew 24:13)

How can we endure under such circumstances? How can we stand firm and not let fear weaken our resolve? It is essential to prepare now. Your Core connection in each battle you fight helps prepare and strengthen you to stand firm to the end. If you have a strong Core connection, drawing from God's strength, wisdom, and love each day, there is a greater chance that you will not give up, but will endure and stand with Christ to the very end.

Chapter 9

NEVER GIVE UP

We are hard pressed on every side, but not crushed; perplexed, but not in despair; persecuted, but not abandoned; struck down, but not destroyed.
2 Corinthians 4:8

Part of Preparing for victory in life's battles is learning to be resilient, and never giving up. As the various battles take place in your life, and the lives of those around you it can be overwhelming if you are not spiritually prepared. All around us there are people who are taking a beating, with little or no time to recover before the battle heats up again. The enemy is relentless. We know he comes to steal, kill and destroy (John 10:10).

Most people are not prepared, they are overcome by the battle, with no weapons of warfare, they lose hope, and give up. But, no matter what, don't quit! Missionary Heidi Baker wisely said, "If you don't quit you win." Don't quit, instead draw closer to God, the Core. That's the right answer no matter what battle you find yourself in. Take time to rest, recover and be restored, but... NEVER GIVE UP! Remember, "... the one who stands firm to the end will be saved." (Matthew 24:13)

DECIDE NOW & SPEAK OUT LOUD:
Giving up is NOT EVER an option!

A great example of resilience is the boxer Rocky Balboa, seen in the "Rocky" movie series. He endures grueling daily training, because he knows the opponent he will face is fierce, and will show no mercy once they are in the ring. So, as he trains and prepares his body, he also trains and prepares his mind to be resilient. When he finally enters the ring, he will have to withstand the attacks of his opponent.

Some matches are easier, and he takes the blows, and comes out with a victory in pretty good shape. But other matches are brutal. He takes blow after blow, but he always gets back up. He never quits. He keeps going. He keeps fighting. That is resilience. That is exactly what we, as Christians, need to learn to do. Take the blows and keep going. Get back up, and never give up. Paul said, "Let us not become weary in doing good, for at the proper time we will reap a harvest if we do not give up." (Galatians 6:9) Keep going. Don't give up.

The enemy has no regard for your age, your knowledge, your title, or your bank account. His only goal is to steal, kill and destroy as many of God's children as possible. That is why we must prepare, we must fight, and we must not ever give up. When one Warrior falls, it affects everyone around them. How can each Warrior remain strong, endure the wages of war, and not give up? You MUST connect to the Core daily. The Core is the source of strength, peace, restoration, guidance, and abundant blessings.

God is the ultimate Spiritual Key. You cannot be overtaken by the enemy if the Holy Spirit resides in you. If you drink from the water of life. Drink in the Holy Spirit and watch God fight for you. Your family needs you. Your friends need you. The lost need Jesus too. Who will tell them? You are not expendable. You are important to God, to your family and friends, and to the many people you can help, love, care for, and bless. Your life is bigger than you can imagine in your own sight. Let God take over and direct you. The reach of your smallest deeds can have eternal blessings.

The Bible tells us, "Be careful how you live and what you believe. NEVER GIVE UP. Then you will save yourself and those who hear you." (1 Timothy 4:16 NIRV emphasis added) Don't miss that first part, "Be careful how you live, and what you believe." The enemy loves to compound and pounce on every struggle. If you are already depressed, the spirit of Depression can come to pull you down further. If you are already stressed or worried, the spirits of Stress and Worry will come to increase intensity. If you are already struggling to hold onto hope, the enemy will come and whisper suicidal thoughts, making them appear like a comfortable solution to all your problems.

THE ENEMY IS A LIAR!!

Do not listen to evil spirits who come to kill you. Do not agree with or entertain them for one moment.

SPEAK OUT LOUD

I plead the blood of Jesus over my household and myself. I bind and cast out the spirits of Depression, Stress, Anxiety, and Suicide. Holy Spirit fill me up and seal off the evil spirits from entering my household or my being ever again. I believe God. I will place my hope in God. He will not fail me. The joy of the Lord is my strength. (Repeat daily and as often as needed)

PERSEVERANCE

Do you not know that in a race all the runners run, but only one gets the prize? Run in such a way as to get the prize. Everyone who competes in the games goes into strict training. They do it to get a crown that will not last, but we do it to get a crown that will last forever. Therefore, I do not run like someone running aimlessly; I do not fight like a boxer beating the air. No, I strike a blow to my body and make it my slave so that after I have preached to others, I myself will not be disqualified for the prize.
- 1 Corinthians 9:24-27

Life is a marathon, not a sprint. There are many uphill battles, but there are also some great downhills. There are obstacles that will block your path, and the enemy will send attacks to take you out before you complete your race. This calls for perseverance and endurance. In the midst of the attacks or the uphill battles it is difficult to imagine making it all the way to the end of the race.

You may grow weary, and tired. But don't lose hope, "Therefore we do not lose heart. Though outwardly we are wasting away, yet inwardly we are being renewed day by day. For our light and momentary troubles are achieving for us an eternal glory that far outweighs them all. So, we fix our eyes not on what is seen, but on what is unseen, since what is seen is temporary, but what is unseen is eternal." (2 Corinthians 4:16-18) The Prepared Warrior learns to fix their eyes on God, not the uphill, not the enemy, not the despair, or even how tired and weary they have become. Any good athlete knows that when you focus on how tired you are, it's harder to keep going. Set your mind and your eyes on God, the Core, and you will be amazed how long you can persevere.

Remember, you are not enduring or persevering alone. There are Christians around the world who are fighting the good fight. There are many who have gone before us, who fought the good fight. Be encouraged, "Therefore, since we are surrounded by such a great cloud of witnesses, let us throw off everything that hinders and the sin that so easily entangles. And let us run with perseverance, the race marked out for us, fixing our eyes on Jesus, the pioneer and perfecter of faith. For the joy set before him he endured the cross, scorning its shame, and sat down at the right hand of the throne of God. Consider him who endured such opposition from sinners, so that you will not grow weary and lose heart." (Hebrews 12:1-3) This amazing verse reminds us to fix our eyes on Jesus and remember all that He endured. When we consider the pain Christ endured for us, it puts our temporary battles in perspective.

Perseverance is closely tied to patience. It can be difficult to be patient in the midst of difficult situations. Our preference will always be for God to move quickly, and preferably at the very beginning of the struggle. But God's ways and his timing are much different than ours. As you get to know God, through reading scripture, you learn that God often waits until the situation looks impossible, and we can see no way out, before moving. When we finally realize, "Only God can save us," then God gets all the glory, and we learn that He will take care of us.

God accomplishes so much just by waiting to move. Not only does He get the full and complete glory and recognition for doing amazing things, he also helps build our faith, and that produces perseverance. James tells us, "Consider it pure joy, my brothers and sisters, whenever you face trials of many kinds, because you know that the testing of your faith produces perseverance. Let perseverance finish its work so that you may be mature and complete, not lacking anything." (James 1:2) God is working even when we're waiting. When God finishes His work in us, we come out of a struggle stronger and more mature.

There are wonderful examples of patience and perseverance in the Bible. Here James points us to the prophets and Job, "Brothers and sisters, as an example of patience in the face of suffering, take the prophets who spoke in the name of the Lord. As you know, we count as blessed those who have persevered. You have heard of Job's perseverance and have seen what the Lord finally brought about. The Lord is full of compassion and mercy." (James 5:10-11) Job's story is one of great suffering. It is a great story for people going through painful periods of life. Job lost as much as any man could, but he still refused to turn from God. Because of his faithfulness and perseverance, "The Lord blessed the latter part of Job's life more than the first." (Job 42:12) God truly is full of compassion and mercy, rewarding those who persevere.

Did you know that there is a reward in heaven for those who persevere? James said, "Blessed is the one who perseveres under trial because, having stood the test, that person will receive the crown of life that the Lord has promised to those who love him." (James 1:12) Like a marathon, just finishing the race may be reward enough! But, after a lifetime of battles, it's just like God to recognize the attribute of persevere with a reward, the crown of life.

Another heavenly reward mentioned in the Bible is the victor's crown. Scripture says, "Do not be afraid of what you are about to suffer. I tell you; the devil will put some of you in prison to test you, and you will suffer persecution for ten days. Be faithful, even to the point of death, and I will give you life as your victor's crown." (Revelation 2:10) Again it is perseverance in battle, overcoming tests and suffering, remaining faithful even until death, that earns the heavenly reward. We must prepare to persevere if we expect to please God and earn His rewards.

Perseverance is necessary for our current battles, and the battles to come. The Bible tells us that as we draw closer to Christ's return the battles will only increase. People of God will be faced with the demand to worship the beast, AKA the Antichrist, and his image, which would condemn them to hell. John says, "This calls for patient endurance on the part of the people of God who keep his commands and remain faithful to Jesus." (Revelation 14:12) How can we possibly be patient or endure under those circumstances, if we are not Preparing now?

How can you grow in faith, patience, and perseverance? Retired Pastor Stan Murdock said it's like building muscles through weightlifting. It takes resistance to build muscle. That same resistance and pressure in the spiritual realm builds our muscles of faith and perseverance. Resistance is necessary for growth. How else will you know God is faithful, unless you are placed in a situation where you have to rely fully on God to help you? Don't give up when you feel the pressure. Endure and persevere, so the pressure builds your spiritual strength. Each battle you endure and persevere through to the end strengthens your spiritual muscles to endure the next battle.

Building perseverance, resilience, and endurance are necessary for every warrior. The apostle Paul wrote this letter to the church in Corinth, to encourage the believers in this way, "… in great endurance; in troubles, hardships and distresses; in beatings, imprisonments and riots; in hard work, sleepless nights and hunger; … with weapons of righteousness in the right hand and in the left; through glory and dishonor, bad report and good report; genuine, yet regarded as impostors; known, yet regarded as unknown; dying, and yet we live on; beaten, and yet not killed; sorrowful, yet always rejoicing; poor, yet making many rich; having nothing, and yet possessing everything." (2 Corinthians 6:4-10) The situation may look dire, but as we press on, we trust God for victory, on earth as it is in Heaven.

COURAGE - NOT FEAR

Preparing for Life's Battles means overcoming a well-known enemy, fear. Fear is a spiritual weapon of the enemy. There is also a spirit of fear that can attach itself to you. Like the other evil spirits, we have discussed, do not listen to or obey the spirit of fear. Cast it out and don't let it back in. God is very clear, "Have I not commanded you? Be strong and courageous. Do not be afraid; do not be discouraged, for the LORD your God will be with you wherever you go." (Joshua 1:9) Paul reminds us, "If God is for us, who can be against us?" (Romans 8:31b)

God isn't the one giving us the spirit of fear, "For you did not receive the spirit of slavery to fall back into fear; but you have received the Spirit of adoption as sons, by whom we cry, 'Abba, Father.'" (Romans 8:15 ESV) No, God has made us sons and daughters who can call on our Father for help!

Crippling fear is from the enemy. There is no place for it in the kingdom of God, "But the cowardly, the unbelieving, the vile, the murderers, the sexually immoral, those who practice magic arts, the idolaters and all liars—they will be consigned to the fiery lake of burning sulfur. This is the second death." (Revelation 21:8) The very first sinners mentioned are the cowards. Cowards are full of fear. But we are not cowards.

We are Prepared Warriors, full of courage! We fear God, and God alone, "Do not be afraid of those who kill the body but cannot kill the soul. Rather, be afraid of the One who can destroy both soul and body in hell." (Matthew 10:28) What you fear has power over you. Only God should have power over us as Christians.

As you spend time with God, in your Core connection, you will come to know Him as all powerful. As He shows up to fight for you in battle, you will realize that the enemy who seems so big to you, is pitiful in his presence. Nothing stands up to God, but all things fall to Him. Once you know these truths, the enemy is no longer something to be afraid of. Once you know your Father is your protector, and He is the most powerful being, you become fearless! God's power and love will heal you of fear, "There is no fear in love. But perfect love drives out fear, because fear has to do with punishment. The one who fears is not made perfect in love." (1 John 4:18)

PRAY OUT LOUD

Father, your word says that perfect love drives out fear. I ask you to cover me and fill me with Your love and remove the spirit of fear from me. Make me courageous, believing you are more powerful than any enemy I will ever face. Nothing stands up to you, but all things fall to you.

WEAPONS & ARMOR

Preparing for battle generally involves some weapons training, and protective armor. Preparing for spiritual battle is no different. We have spiritual weapons, "For though we live in the world, we do not wage war as the world does. The weapons we fight with are not the weapons of the world. On the contrary, they have divine power to demolish strongholds. We demolish arguments and every pretension that sets itself up against the knowledge of God, and we take captive every thought to make it obedient to Christ. And we will be ready to punish every act of disobedience, once your obedience is complete." (2 Corinthians 10:3-6) Yes, we have weapons, the first and most important weapon we will discuss in this book is the Core connection.

Spending time with God in His Word, Worship, and Prayer are powerful weapons. They may not seem powerful right now. You may not understand how those three things can possibly be weapons let alone protect you. But as you take up your arms and begin to use them, you will find they are more powerful than you ever imagined. The protective armor of God is necessary for success in battle. It is important to put it on daily, before you even start your day.

> *Put on the full armor of God, so that you can take your stand against the devil's schemes. For our struggle is not against flesh and blood, but against the rulers, against the authorities, against the powers of this dark world and against the spiritual forces of evil in the heavenly realms. Therefore, put on the full armor of God, so that when the day of evil comes, you may be able to stand your ground, and after you have done everything, to stand. Stand firm then, with the belt of truth buckled around your waist, with the breastplate of righteousness in place, and with your feet fitted with the readiness that comes from the gospel of peace. In addition to all this, take up the shield of faith, with which you can extinguish all the flaming arrows of the evil one. Take the helmet of salvation and the sword of the Spirit, which is the word of God. And pray in the Spirit on all occasions with all kinds of prayers and requests. With this in mind, be alert and always keep on praying for all the saints.*
> *- Ephesians 6:10-18*

Our weapons and armor are closely tied together. Like any warrior, your armor can also be used as a weapon. There is more to come on this topic! We prepare for battle, knowing it will surely come, but we face it with courage; prepared to be resilient and persevere, by connecting to the Core, God, daily.

Chapter 10

PREPARE FOR JUDGMENT DAY

God will bring into judgment both the righteous and the wicked,
for there will be a time for every activity, a time to judge every deed.
Ecclesiastes 3:17

Our final goal is to help warriors prepare for Judgment Day. This is the most important aspect of being a Prepared Warrior. Even if you struggle through victories in life's battles, your preparation for Judgment Day holds eternal consequences or blessings. So, don't miss this. Don't skip this. Certainly, don't devalue the importance of this section.

Imagine you are taking a very important class. The teacher informs the class, through a letter, that the final exam at the end of the school year will determine if you pass or fail the class. Within the letter, the teacher gives the students all they need to know to pass the final exam. Step one is to know the teacher. If you show up for the exam, and it's the first time the teacher has ever seen you, and doesn't know you, it's an automatic fail for the class. However, should you show up for the exam and the teacher embraces you, as good friends do, you pass the exam.

Jesus is the teacher and judgment day is the final exam. The best way to prepare for judgment day is to know and have a relationship with Jesus. There is a lot more to this section, and a lot more to explore. But, if you remember nothing else, remember this first point: **The best way to prepare for Judgment Day is to know Jesus and have a relationship with Him.**

Bible prophecy, and Jesus himself reveals that He will return. But whether Christ's return or death reaches you first, we all must face what awaits on Judgment Day. The Bible holds many scriptures that give us a glimpse into what is to come after this life. We know for sure that judgment awaits all of us, "For we must all appear before the judgment seat of Christ, so that each of us may receive what is due us for the things done while in the body, whether good or bad." (2 Corinthians 5:10) We will all come before God to give an account for our lives. It is essential that you have accepted Jesus before you get there. Jesus is the key to eternity in heaven. But what you do after you choose Jesus also holds eternal consequence or blessing. Let's Prepare now, so when the day arrives, we are ready to meet our Maker.

DEATH

There are two possible ways you will exit this life, Christ's return or death. The majority of mankind will be taken by death. Most people don't like to talk or even think about it. It can be scary because there is so much uncertainty involved in when it will happen, how it will happen, etc. However, when you have the Core connection, you know and love Jesus, and death is no longer something you fear.

Love conquers fear, "There is no fear in love. But perfect love drives out fear, because fear has to do with punishment. The one who fears is not made perfect in love." (1 John 4:18) The more you love and cherish Jesus, the less fear you will have in your life, including fear of death. The more you love Jesus, the more you will trust Him to care for you in your moment of death, and beyond death.

Why can you trust Jesus to care for you beyond death? Because Jesus has conquered death. First, during Jesus' ministry on earth He raised the dead back to life. He raised Lazarus (John 11), Jairus' daughter (Mark 5), and the widow's son (Luke 7). Then, after Jesus suffered his own gruesome and painful death, He himself came back to life. His resurrection was witnessed by hundreds of people. It was and is still a key point to our faith in Christ, because it fulfilled prophecy, and confirmed His deity.

Who else, but God could overcome death on their own? The early Christian, Timothy, said, "… our Savior, Christ Jesus, who has destroyed death and has brought life and immortality to light through the gospel." (2 Timothy 1:10) Jesus is the only key figure of any religion who defeated death. All others are still in the grave. But, Jesus said, "I am the Living One; I was dead, and now look, I am alive for ever and ever! And I hold the keys of death and Hades." (Revelation 1:18) Jesus holds the keys! Jesus is the to victory over death!

CHRIST'S RETURN

Christ's return is another possible way you could exit this life. The Bible prophesies His eminent return, "Look, he is coming with the clouds," and "every eye will see him, even those who pierced him." (Revelation 1:7) When Jesus Christ returns every eye will see Him, it will not be a secret. He will return as the victor, "For the Lord himself will come down from heaven, with a loud command, with the voice of the archangel and with the trumpet call of God, and the dead in Christ will rise first. After that, we who are still alive and are left will be caught up together with them in the clouds to meet the Lord in the air. And so, we will be with the Lord forever." (1 Thessalonians 4:16-17) When Christ returns, He is coming to take His followers with Him. Wouldn't that be amazing to be part of that awesome experience!

The Bible doesn't tell us when He will return, "But about that day or hour no one knows, not even the angels in heaven, nor the Son, but only the Father." (Matthew 24:36) However, we are told to keep watch, "Therefore keep watch, because you do not know on what day your Lord will come. But understand this: If the owner of the house had known at what time of night the thief was coming, he would have kept watch and would not have let his house be broken into. So, you also must be ready, because the Son of Man will come at an hour when you do not expect him." (Matthew 24:42-44) We need to be ready and prepared for Christ's Return.

We must prepare, even as we patiently wait for His return, "Be patient, then, brothers and sisters, until the Lord's coming. See how the farmer waits for the land to yield its valuable crop, patiently waiting for the autumn and spring rains. You too, be patient and stand firm, because the Lord's coming is near. Don't grumble against one another, brothers and sisters, or you will be judged. The Judge is standing at the door!" (James 5:7)

If you entered a courtroom, you would want to be ready to face the Judge and have all your paperwork in order. You want the best possible outcome in the courtroom. With that in mind, preparing to meet God, the true and final Judge, is of even greater importance. His verdict is absolute, and no further arguments or appeals are allowed.

JUDGMENT

In Matthew 25 we get a very clear picture of the judgment that will take place when Christ returns, "When the Son of Man comes in his glory, and all the angels with him, he will sit on his glorious throne. All the nations will be gathered before him, and he will separate the people one from another as a shepherd separates the sheep from the goats. He will put the sheep on his right and the goats on his left. Then the King will say to those on his right, 'Come, you who are blessed by my Father; take your inheritance, the kingdom prepared for you since the creation of the world." (Matthew 25:31-34)

There is clearly a separation that will take place. Those called sheep, on the right, will inherit the kingdom of God. Those on the left, the goats, are told, "Depart from me, you who are cursed, into the eternal fire prepared for the devil and his angels." (Matthew 25:41) The first part of the judgment will be determining who will enter the kingdom of God, and who will be sent to hell.

It is important to note again that Jesus is the key. The Bible says of the new Heaven, "Nothing impure will ever enter it, nor will anyone who does what is shameful or deceitful, but only those whose names are written in the Lamb's book of life." (Revelation 21:27) Notice your name must be in, "the Lamb's book of life." The Lamb is Jesus. It's His book. He is the key.

It is also important to note, "the Father judges no one, but has entrusted all judgment to the Son." (John 5:22) The Son is Jesus. He is the judge. He is the key. You can't skip over Jesus and expect it to go well for you on judgment day. Without Jesus it will be quite the opposite, "Anyone whose name was not found written in the book of life was thrown into the lake of fire." (Revelation 20:15)

Without Jesus, we are subject to pay for our sins, right along with the rest of the sinners, "But the cowardly, the unbelieving, the vile, the murderers, the sexually immoral, those who practice magic arts, the idolaters and all liars—they will be consigned to the fiery lake of burning sulfur. This is the second death." (Revelation 21:8) Sin is serious, and it results in death. Jesus is essential to pay for our sins, and so remove the penalty of death.

Jesus also gives us a glimpse of judgment day in Matthew 25:31-46. In this passage Jesus instructs us to take care of "the least of these" or people who are hungry, thirsty, needing clothes, strangers, sick, or in prison. Then, Jesus takes it a step further, "Not everyone who says to me, 'Lord, Lord,' will enter the kingdom of heaven, but only the one who does the will of my Father who is in heaven." (Matthew 7:21) So, Jesus expects His followers to do the will of God the Father. It's not simply enough to just believe Jesus is the son of God, even Satan believes that! He goes on to say, "Many will say to me on that day, 'Lord, Lord, did we not prophesy in your name and in your name drive out demons and in your name perform many miracles?' Then I will tell them plainly, 'I never knew you. Away from me, you evildoers.'" (Matthew 7:22-23) It is more important for us to know Jesus, and do the will of the Father, then perform all the other works.

For that reason, we are starting here, with the Core connection. Spending time with God is the most important thing you can do. It is the most important part of being a Prepared Warrior and Preparing for Judgment Day. As you make your Core connection a priority, all the other pieces will fall into place. Jesus said, "But seek first his kingdom and his righteousness, and all these things will be given to you as well." (Matthew 6:33) When we spend time with God, His Holy Spirit counsels you, aligns you with His will and purpose for you, and provides for all of your needs.

HEAVENLY REWARDS

In order to prepare for Judgment Day, it's good to know what to expect. There is more to Christ's return than judgment of sins, there is also something glorious for those who love Christ, rewards! Most people are familiar with God's judgment and heaven and hell, but what you may not know is that God gives glorious rewards! In heaven there will be a review of your life on earth, "The dead were judged according to what they had done as recorded in the books." (Revelation 20:12b) The Bible also says, "I the LORD search the heart and examine the mind, to reward each person according to their conduct, according to what their deeds deserve." (Jeremiah 17:10) Jesus uses a parable in Matthew 25 and Luke 12 to help us understand what He expects of us.

The first one is the Parable of the Ten Virgins. (Matthew 25:1-13) Here we see two sets of virgins, five foolish, and five wise. The wise virgins are prepared to meet their bridegroom. They made sure their lamps had enough oil. The foolish virgins were not prepared and let the oil in their lamps get low. In this parable Jesus uses the example of brides (virgin), waiting for their groom (bridegroom), just as the Christians await Christ's return.

Jesus said, "the bridegroom was a long time in coming, and they all became drowsy and fell asleep." (Matthew 25:5) Likewise, many Christians today have fallen asleep and failed to prepare for Christ's return. These are the foolish virgins (foolish Christians). Then, when Christ returns, they won't have enough oil and miss His return. How do we get enough oil? Spending time with God daily, in Core connection. Those who were prepared received the reward of going to the wedding banquet (a celebration in heaven).

The second one is the Parable of the Bags of Gold. (Matthew 25:14-30) In this story there are three servants who are each given various amounts of gold from their master. When the master returns, he expects to see it increased. The first and second servants were found faithful and increased the amount of gold for the master. The third servant was fearful and hid his gold in the ground. The master was angry with the third servant, and he was cast into the darkness. But the first and second servants received rewards.

Likewise, each of us are given gifts from God. He expects us to use and multiply them before he returns. Jesus said, "everyone who has been given much, much will be demanded; and from the one who has been entrusted with much, much more will be asked." (Luke 12: 48b) If we are faithful with all God entrusts us with, we can hope to hear the Lord say, as the master said to his first and second servants, "Well done, good and faithful servant! You have been faithful with a few things; I will put you in charge of many things. Come and share your master's happiness!" (Matthew 25:21) Those who are found faithful will be rewarded and receive an increase in God's kingdom.

We see from these two parables that God will reward those who are prepared for Christ's return, and have been found faithful with all that was entrusted to them. But that's not all! The Bible says, "Blessed are you when people hate you, when they exclude you and insult you and reject your name as evil, because of the Son of Man. Rejoice on that day and leap for joy, because great is your reward in heaven. For that is how their ancestors treated the prophets." (Luke 6:22-23) Did you know there are rewards for you when you suffer because of Jesus? What a comfort to know that God sees your pain and will bless you for it.

All who long for Christ's appearing are assured to be rewarded a crown of righteousness, "I have fought the good fight, I have finished the race, I have kept the faith. Now there is in store for me the crown of righteousness, which the Lord, the righteous Judge, will award to me on that day—and not only to me, but also to all who have longed for his appearing."

(2 Timothy 4:7-8) If we long for his appearance we will be rewarded. We can do that! It is especially easy to long for his appearance if we are prepared for Christ's return!

There are rewards for Christian leaders and teachers who have faithfully served and cared for their flock, "And when the Chief Shepherd appears, you will receive the crown of glory that will never fade away." (1 Peter 5:4) The rewards of heaven never fade away.

There are rewards for those who are victorious, "The one who is victorious will, like them, be dressed in white. I will never blot out the name of that person from the book of life, but will acknowledge that name before my Father and his angels." (Revelation 3:5) There are many more rewards mentioned in scripture.

All God's rewards will be amazing, "What no eye has seen, what no ear has heard, and what no human mind has conceived —the things God has prepared for those who love him—" (1 Corinthians 2:9) As those who follow and love Christ, it should be every Christian's greatest desire to hear, "Well done my good and faithful servant." The rewards are just an added bonus for pleasing our Father and doing His will.

Revelation holds a beautiful picture of those who received heavenly rewards, "the twenty-four elders fall down before him who sits on the throne and worship him who lives for ever and ever. They lay their crowns before the throne and say: 'You are worthy, our Lord and God, to receive glory and honor and power, for you created all things, and by your will they were created and have their being.'" (Revelation 4:10-11) After receiving their rewards, the elders gave them right back to the King, honoring God.

But, in our quest to gain heavenly rewards, heed this warning from Jesus, "Be careful not to practice your righteousness in front of others to be seen by them. If you do, you will have no reward from your Father in heaven. So, when you give to the needy, do not announce it with trumpets, as the hypocrites do in the synagogues and on the streets, to be honored by others. Truly I tell you, they have received their reward in full. But when you give to the needy, do not let your left hand know what your right hand is doing, so that your giving may be in secret. Then your Father, who sees what is done in secret, will reward you. And when you pray, do not be like the hypocrites, for they love to pray standing in the synagogues and on the street corners to be seen by others. Truly I tell you, they have received their reward in full. But when you pray, go into your room, close the door and pray to your Father, who is unseen. Then your Father, who sees what is done in secret, will reward you." (Matthew 6:1-6)

Jesus also told them, "When you fast, do not look somber as the hypocrites do, for they disfigure their faces to show others they are fasting. Truly I tell you, they have received their reward in full. But when you fast, put oil on your head and wash your face, so that it will not be obvious to others that you are fasting, but only to your Father, who is unseen; and your Father, who sees what is done in secret, will reward you." (Matthew 6:16-18) Are you seeing the pattern here? God doesn't want us to do righteous acts, like prayer, giving to the needy, and fasting, in front of other people. Pride and self-righteousness may creep in. But if we do them in secret, God says He will reward us in heaven.

The kingdom of God is so opposite of how our earthly kingdom operates. Here we give awards for accomplishments, making the most money, being the most beautiful, being the best athlete or artist, being the most popular or well liked. But God's awards are different, "And everyone who has left houses or brothers or sisters or father or mother or wife or children or fields for my sake will receive a hundred times as much and will inherit eternal life. But many who are first will be last, and many who are last will be first.'" (Matthew 19:29-30)

God sees everything different. It is wise to read and learn about the kingdom of God, and what He expects from us. If we only follow what the world says, we will not be prepared on judgment day. If we follow what God says, we are assured a glorious entrance into His kingdom!

PREPARED WARRIORS

Prepared Warriors of all ages and all levels are set to prepare for life's battles and judgment day. Victory is assured for Prepared Warriors because they serve under the King of all Kings. God is a fierce warrior, who has never been, and will never be defeated! The enemy's attack is futile as they will always lose to God. Nothing stands up to Him, but all things fall to Him.

Battles are all around, internal, external, and territorial, but the Warriors are prepared. They are resilient and never give up! The warriors persevere and are full of courage. They use every weapon of warfare and have impenetrable armor. Prepared Warriors will be ready for Judgment Day! They do not fear death, because Christ holds the key to death and hades. The warriors are wise, and prepared. They have multiplied everything God gave them. Warriors know what is important to God and His kingdom and are sure to receive abundant heavenly rewards.

**Prepared Warriors are spiritually prepared
for life's battles and judgment day**

THE CORE

74

PART 3

CORE CONNECTION

Chapter 11

TJ'S STORY
DISTRACTIONS & TRAPS

The demons clustered at a safe distance, awaiting a word from the head demon assigned to TJ. In deep thought, he turned his back to the other demons. He knew his assignment well. It is the same assignment for every Christian: knock them down, get them off track, keep them from getting closer to God, discovering their purpose, and power they now possessed, as children of God. He also knew if he wasn't successful, he would have hell to pay when his superior returned.

Now to decide which tactic to use. It's best to hit his target on multiple fronts. If he can get TJ overwhelmed with attacks, he may just surrender. But there is something extremely satisfying about a subtle attack, planting a lie and watching it grow into complete deception. There were many different plans going through the demon's mind. A decision had to be made soon. A new Christian left unchecked could quickly become a major problem beyond his own territory. He couldn't let that happen.

As for TJ's time at school, the other kids were already well trained, and TJ seemed powerless to stop their attacks. That plan was working out nicely. It also had an unanticipated effect with the other Christian students. They shrunk into the background every time one of their fellow Christians was being attacked. They had no interest in drawing the attacks upon themselves.

At home TJ and his mom had settled into the routine of their daily coming and going. Both were too busy for any meaningful time to talk. TJ had already shared Jesus with her. She just didn't seem interested. This delighted the demons. They didn't even need to set a trap or make a plan. TJ's mom was far too preoccupied with her own thoughts, and the demons of Worry and Stress interjecting as needed.

With those areas covered, the demons just had one area left to disrupt, TJ's thirst for learning about God. The more TJ studied the Word of God, the more he realized he had so much to learn. He felt like he was playing catch up with all the kids who had been in Sunday School class since birth! It was a bit overwhelming. But TJ knew he was headed in the right direction and was motivated to start searching out new sources of information. There were tons of videos on the internet, podcasts, radio programs, books, and websites. But TJ had already been warned to be careful who he followed, so he was cautious. There are a lot of false teachers and religions out there. Some are even very close to Christianity. How could TJ know what was true and what was false?

TJ talked things over with Teyo and they knew he needed some guidance, and someone who could help answer questions for him. After some discussion they agreed Mark, the youth group leader at the church, seemed to have a lot of knowledge, and seemed willing to answer questions. So, he decided to start there. TJ asked Mark for a list of some good books to read and good teachers he recommended. Mark was happy to help, and quickly put together a list.

TJ went to the library, but they didn't carry any of the books. Then, he went online to look up the teachers. TJ's angel watched contently while TJ listened to a teacher who said, "If you want to know God, you need to spend time with Him." It never occurred to TJ that he could spend time with God. He can't even see God. How does that even work? As TJ listened, the teacher spelled out three ways to spend time with God: reading God's Word, worshiping and prayer. That seemed simple enough.

The head demon let out an angry roar and sent the smaller demons near him flying through the air, "I told you to alert me if he started searching! I asked to know his every move! We had a small window to plant a lie, to get him off track and we missed it! Now he is listening to these teachers who know God's word! They know the power they possess, and they will teach TJ! How could this happen? I can't leave my post for a moment without you messing it up! I will have to just do this all myself!" With that the demon headed straight for TJ's house. He had a lot of work to do, and just a little time.

Upon the demon's arrival, he was confronted with the object of his scorn. TJ, with his ever-present angel, had quickly become a thorn in his side. TJ was watching a video from a well-known, highly respected, Christian teacher. This teacher had proved to be a worthy adversary, and difficult to bring down, even by the higher-ranking demons. This would not end well. He would have to put a stop to this immediately! What could he do? TJ's ever vigilant angel was already aware of his presence, and he couldn't lay a finger on him!

Then, the thought came to him, the Internet was filled with vile and sexual images. He just needed one image to pop up and draw TJ astray. That wouldn't be hard. There were multitudes of demons working to ensure these images populate every person's computer, phone and screen. The demon quickly made contact with the spirits of Lust and Pornography, and the trap was laid. It was simple really. The plan of drawing TJ into sin, would draw him away from God. It works every time.

With that final piece the demons congratulated themselves on a job well done. They felt very confident they had all their bases covered with TJ. No threats here.

THE CORE

Chapter 12

THE CORE

Imagine you are taking a class to learn about the President of the United States. While the teacher is talking, the President walks into your class! But instead of acknowledging that the person you are talking about is actually in the room with you, the teacher keeps teaching. Then, you read a book about the President, while he waits quietly in the seat next to you. After that, you watch a video about the President, trying to learn as much as you can about him. BUT THE PRESIDENT IS RIGHT NEXT TO YOU!! This is what happens all too often in our lives. We study God, but don't have a relationship with Him. All of the wonderful Christian resources in the world, including this book, cannot replace actually talking to God, or spending time with Him.

Seeking and finding God for the sake of relationship is the highest honor and reward of every person and Prepared Warrior. The amazing honor of being able to connect with the Creator of the entire universe and every living thing is beyond reason. Think about how difficult it would be to get a meeting with the leader of a major company, or government official. Yet, God, who is infinitely higher than all earthly leaders, kings and rulers, desires time alone with you each day.

As you already discovered "the Core" is God. Referring to God as the Core is not meant in any way to diminish who He is, but to give you a visual focus and understanding of His placement in our lives. God is our focus, our center, our source. The definition of Core is a central and often foundational part usually distinct from the enveloping part by a difference in nature. (Merriam-Webster Dictionary) God truly is the center and foundation of everything.

God is the Core, the source for every good thing, "Every good and perfect gift is from above, coming down from the Father of the heavenly lights, who does not change like shifting shadows." (James 1:17) We can trust that God is the same yesterday, today and tomorrow.

He already holds infinite wisdom; He has no need to grow, change, or evolve. He is not like us, "God is not man, that He should lie, or a son of man, that He should change His mind. Does He speak and not act? Does He promise and not fulfill?" (Numbers 23:19) We cannot diminish God to our own human character. God said, through the prophet Isaiah, "'For my thoughts are not your thoughts, neither are your ways my ways,' declares the Lord. 'For as the heavens are higher than the earth, so my ways are higher than your ways and my thoughts than your thought.'" (Isaiah 55:8-9) God is so great. Who can understand all his ways?

God expressed His grandeur when He spoke to Job, "Who is this that obscures my plans with words without knowledge?" (Job 38:2) Even the best and brightest human minds pale in comparison to the Creator, "But God chose the foolish things of the world to shame the wise; God chose the weak things of the world to shame the strong. God chose the lowly things of this world and the despised things – and the things that are not – to nullify the things that are, so that no one may boast before him." (1 Corinthians 1:27-30) Those who truly know God, are humbled before Him.

The complexity and awesomeness of God is beyond our understanding; there is no earthly way to comprehend all that He is. Yet, through His Word, He gives us a guide to understand Him better. We can see how He acted in the past. How He interacted and responded to His people. We can read the words He spoke through the prophets. We can see His great love for us, His amazing grace and mercy, through the story of Jesus Christ. Yes, God desires to reveal Himself to His people. He desires a relationship with us. When Jesus was asking which commandment in the law was the greatest, "Jesus replied: 'Love the Lord your God with all your heart and with all your soul and with all your mind.' This is the first and greatest command.'" (Matt 22:37-38) Loving God is the most important command we can follow. Through a loving relationship, God can help guide us to become the people He created us to be. Through a loving relationship, we can also learn and understand more about God, our Creator.

HOLY TRINITY

So, now let's talk about God. The term "God" encompasses the Holy Trinity: God the Father, the Son (Jesus), and the Holy Spirit. God is one being with three parts. Christians do not worship three Gods. There is only one God. Just like water can take different forms like ice, liquid, or steam, and still be water. God has different forms but is still all one God. God the Father has a Spirit, the Holy Spirit. His Spirit is complex, pliable, and dividable. The Holy Spirit resides in the Father, the Son (Jesus), and also outside of a being.

Miraculously, each person who accepts Christ, is also filled with the Holy Spirit. Our bodies hold our own unique spirits; you are still you. But when you accept Christ, His Spirit also comes and lives in you. The Holy Spirit is what God uses to connect Himself to everyone in His kingdom around the world. It's really quite an amazing communication and power system.

What separates Jesus from us, and what makes Him God, is that He also has God's DNA. The angel told Mary she would have a child, though she was a virgin, "The Holy Spirit will come on you, and the power of the Most High will overshadow you. So, the holy one to be born will be called the Son of God." (Luke 1:35) When Jesus died on the cross, God the Father was still on the throne in Heaven, the Holy Spirit was still alive and active. Jesus alone suffered and died. His human body endured pain and death for us, the ultimate sacrifice as payment for our sin. But because He is God, Jesus overcame death. The Holy Spirit inhabited His body, healing and restoring His body.

The Father, the Son, and the Spirit are one God. Jesus said, "Anyone who has seen me has seen the Father. How can you say, 'Show us the Father'? Don't you believe that I am in the Father, and that the Father is in me? The words I say to you I do not speak on my own authority. Rather, it is the Father, living in me, who is doing his work. Believe me when I say that I am in the Father and the Father is in me." (John 14:9-11)

For true Core connection, it is important to grasp the unique parts of the Holy Trinity of God. Each part of God holds truth and information about who He is. Each part, aspect and attribute of God is worthy of worship and praise.

GOD THE FATHER

God the Father sits on the throne in Heaven, "At once I was in the Spirit, and there before me was a throne in heaven with someone sitting on it. And the one who sat there had the appearance of jasper and ruby. A rainbow that shone like an emerald encircled the throne." (Revelation 4:2-3).

- His power and authority are beyond our understanding, "For the Lord Most High is awesome, the great King over all the earth." (Psalm 47:2) He reigns over all the earth and every nation, "God reigns over the nations; God is seated on his holy throne." (Psalm 47:8)
- God is the creator, "You alone are the LORD. You made the heavens, even the highest heavens, and all their starry hosts, the earth and all that is on it, the seas and all that is in them. You give life to everything, and the multitudes of heaven worship you." (Nehemiah 9:6)
- God is our Father, "one God and Father of all, who is over all and through all and in all." (Ephesians 4:6) He is a kind and compassionate Father, "A father to the fatherless, a defender of widows, is God in his holy dwelling. God sets the lonely in families, he leads out the prisoners with singing." (Psalm 68: 5-6)

- God is faithful and full of love, "Know therefore that the Lord your God is God; he is the faithful God, keeping his covenant of love to a thousand generations of those who love him and keep his commands." (Deuteronomy 7:9)
- God is above all things, "For the Lord your God is God of gods and Lord of lords, the great God, mighty and awesome, who shows no partiality and accepts no bribes." (Deuteronomy 10:17)

This is just a quick glimpse into who God, the Father, is. Daily Core connection is essential to fully know Him. It is an unending quest.

GOD THE SON

Jesus is the son of God, "We know also that the Son of God has come and has given us understanding, so that we may know him who is true. And we are in him who is true by being in his Son Jesus Christ. He is the true God and eternal life." (1 John 5:20)

The Bible tells us, Jesus "The Son is the radiance of God's glory and the exact representation of his being, sustaining all things by his powerful word. After he had provided purification for sins, he sat down at the right hand of the Majesty in heaven. So, he became as much superior to the angels as the name he has inherited is superior to theirs." (Hebrews 1:3-4)

- Jesus came to save us from our sins, by dying on the cross, "In fact, the law requires that nearly everything be cleansed with blood, and without the shedding of blood there is no forgiveness." (Hebrews 9:22)
- Jesus came so we can have life, "Whoever has the Son has life; whoever does not have the Son of God does not have life." (1 John 5:12)
- Jesus is the great mediator, "For there is one God and one mediator between God and mankind, the man Christ Jesus." (1 Timothy 2:5)
- Jesus is our High Priest. In the Bible the High Priest entered the temple's Most Holy Place every year to make atonement for the sins of the people. But Jesus paid the price once and for all, "So Christ was sacrificed once to take away the sins of many; and he will appear a second time, not to bear sin, but to bring salvation to those who are waiting for him." (Hebrews 9:28)
- Jesus is returning again, to save His people from this fallen world, "Look, he is coming with the clouds, and 'every eye will see him, even those who pierced him,' and all peoples on earth 'will mourn because of him.' So, shall it be! Amen." (Revelation 1:7)

This is just a quick glimpse into who Jesus, the Son of God, is. Daily Core connection is essential to fully know Him. It is an unending quest.

GOD THE HOLY SPIRIT

The Holy Spirit is the Spirit of God. His Spirit was there at the beginning of the world, "Now the earth was formless and empty, darkness was over the surface of the deep, and the Spirit of God was hovering over the waters." (Genesis 1:2)

- The Holy Spirit lives within us, "Do you not know that your bodies are temples of the Holy Spirit, who is in you, whom you have received from God? You are not your own;" (1 Corinthians 6:19)
- The Holy Spirit is always with us; we are not alone, "And I will ask the Father, and he will give you another advocate to help you and be with you forever— the Spirit of truth. The world cannot accept him, because it neither sees him nor knows him. But you know him, for he lives with you and will be in you. I will not leave you as orphans; I will come to you." (John 14:14-18)
- The Holy Spirit leads us and guides His children, "For those who are led by the Spirit of God are the children of God." (Romans 8:14)

The Holy Spirit helps us and intercedes for us, "In the same way, the Spirit helps us in our weakness. We do not know what we ought to pray for, but the Spirit himself intercedes for us through wordless groans. And he who searches our hearts knows the mind of the Spirit, because the Spirit intercedes for God's people in accordance with the will of God." (Romans 8:26-27)

The Holy Spirit reveals the thoughts of God to us, "these are the things God has revealed to us by his Spirit. The Spirit searches all things, even the deep things of God. For who knows a person's thoughts except their own spirit within them? In the same way no one knows the thoughts of God except the Spirit of God. What we have received is not the spirit of the world, but the Spirit who is from God, so that we may understand what God has freely given us. This is what we speak, not in words taught us by human wisdom but in words taught by the Spirit, explaining spiritual realities with Spirit-taught words. The person without the Spirit does not accept the things that come from the Spirit of God but considers them foolishness, and cannot understand them because they are discerned only through the Spirit. The person with the Spirit makes judgments about all things, but such a person is not subject to merely human judgments, for, 'Who has known the mind of the Lord so as to instruct him? But we have the mind of Christ.'" (1 Corinthians 2:10-16)

Jesus spoke about the Holy Spirit, "But when he, the Spirit of truth, comes, he will guide you into all the truth. He will not speak on his own; he will speak only what he hears, and he will tell you what is yet to come. He will glorify me because it is from me that he will receive what he will make known to you. All that belongs to the Father is mine. That is why I said the Spirit will receive from me what he will make known to you." (John 16:13-15)

This is just a quick glimpse into who God, the Holy Spirit, is. Daily Core connection is essential to fully know Him. It is an unending quest.

God is more complex than we are. We cannot simplify Him down to our own likeness. We are created in His image, but we are not a copy. God is the Father in Heaven, who sits on the throne, the Creator of the Universe. God also came to earth as a man, yet holding the Spirit of God within. God's Spirit is not contained in one being, as ours is. He defies limitations. Learning who God really is, and learning the truth, is a journey worth taking. The closer you get to God, the greater peace you will have. God is the truth, the source, and the Core we desire to connect to.

Chapter 13

CORE CONNECTION

God is not hiding; He is waiting. He is waiting for you to seek Him, "You will seek me and find me when you seek me with all your heart. I will be found by you," declares the LORD." (Jeremiah 29:13-14) God is faithful to be found. But God is a gentleman. He doesn't push himself on anyone. If you want Him in your life, He will be there. If you won't want Him in your life, He will move out. You choose. It is true that if you, "Draw near to God and He will draw near to you." (James 4:8) It's that simple.

There are three elements to Core connection: The Word of God, Worship, and Prayer. The next chapters will detail how to use these three elements to seek and draw near to God. Each element is important for different reasons. Collectively they work together to produce a well-rounded, fully developed Core connection.

A Prepared Warrior is much like an athlete who competes in triathlons trains in three areas: running, biking, and swimming. They are physically prepared to conquer each physical challenge. The Prepared Warrior, who trains in the Word, Worship, and Prayer is more spiritually prepared to conquer in spiritual challenges.

Also, like an athlete who is strong in running, swimming may be more of a challenge. Each person has an area of spiritual strength. Maybe your area of strength is in prayer; that doesn't mean the other areas should be ignored. It benefits you to put concerted effort into your area(s) of weakness, and become a well-rounded, fully trained, spiritual warrior.

All of these elements are free, and available to every person on earth. It won't cost you any money or require tools you don't have. The path to God isn't just for the wealthy or the well-educated. It is not for the elite, or just the chosen people. God made himself accessible to all people. It will only cost you your time.

As you move into Core connection, you must understand the rule of sowing and reaping. If you seek God a little bit, you will receive a little bit. If you seek God with all your heart, you will receive Him in abundance. The more you put into your relationship with God, the more you will get out of it. When you spend time with God, He will multiply your time. When you give your money to God, He will multiply your money. Whatever you sacrifice, or give, to God, He will multiply. So, no time with God is ever wasted time.

The greatest benefit of Core connection is building your relationship with God. It is the highest honor that God sees and loves you, and desires to spend time with you. Though the blessings and gifts you receive from Him are amazing, they are just fringe benefits of being in relationship with Him.

Imagine if you had access to a powerful King. You sent him an invitation to meet, and He accepted. But when you arrived, instead of talking with the King, and desiring to know Him, you simply asked for the gifts within His Kingdom. In His graciousness and kindness, He may grant you the gifts you requested, but ultimately you missed out on the greatest gift, knowing the King.

The Core connection calls us to prioritize and focus on knowing the King. There are many steps for the Prepared Warrior to follow after the Core connection, but the Core connection is the most important. Many of your battles will be fought and won at the feet of the King, without even having to mention the battle to Him.

I keep asking that the God of our Lord Jesus Christ, the glorious Father, may give you the Spirit of wisdom and revelation, so that you may know him better. I pray that the eyes of your heart may be enlightened in order that you may know the hope to which he has called you, the riches of his glorious inheritance in his holy people. - Ephesians 1:17-18

When our eyes are on God, amazing things happen. When our eyes are on the enemy, that's when fear, worry, and depression creep in. But, when we start by connecting to God, and keep our eyes on Him, we will have victory in our battles. It's really amazing how God works. This ties back to the rule of sowing and reaping. When we sow our time into God, we spend less time in battle. When we sow our time into God, we don't have to strive or fight as hard. God fights for us! God tells us which battles to fight. God gives us the battle strategy. God is our protector in battle. For these reasons, we must connect to the Core, before we go to war!

Amazing things happen when you spend time with God. God gives you life to the fullest! God is everything, in the literal sense of the word. He is Almighty God, who sustains your life daily. He allows you to have breath, He allows your heart to beat, He allows you to live. God provides every good and perfect gift. (James 1:17) He is your provider, your healer, your counselor, your best friend, your Father, and your God. Jesus explained the Core connection like connecting a branch to the vine, "I am the vine; you are the branches. If you remain in me and I in you, you will bear much fruit; apart from me you can do nothing." (John 15:5) The connection is essential for life and to bear fruit. A branch that is not attached to the vine will not produce fruit, it will wither and die. If you had to gauge your connection level right now, what would it be?

LEVEL OF CORE CONNECTION

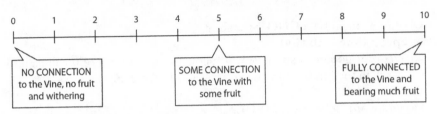

FRUIT OF CONNECTION

By the time you finish this book, you will be equipped to become fully connected to the Vine and bearing much fruit. The more time you spend with God, the more like God you will become, and the more fruit you will produce. The Bible says the fruit of His Spirit, or what His Spirit produces and brings forth is, "...love, joy, peace, patience, kindness, goodness, faithfulness, gentleness and self-control." (Galatians 5:22-23 ESV)

Do you want true, everlasting, unconditional LOVE?
-- Spend time with God.
"I have loved you with an everlasting love; I have drawn you with unfailing kindness." (Jeremiah 31:3)

Do you want JOY instead of sorrow and heartache?
-- Spend time with God.
"May the God of hope fill you with all joy and peace as you trust in him, so that you may overflow with hope by the power of the Holy Spirit." (Romans 15:13)

Do you desperately want your spirit to be at PEACE?
-- Spend time with God.
"I have told you these things, so that in me you may have peace. In this world you will have trouble. But take heart! I have overcome the world." (John 16:33)

Do you need to be more PATIENT with those around you?
-- Spend time with God.
"The Lord is not slow in keeping his promise, as some understand slowness.

Instead he is patient with you, not wanting anyone to perish, but everyone to come into repentance." (2 Peter 3:9)

Do you want to be a KIND person?
-- Spend time with God.
"Be kind and compassionate to one another, forgiving each other, just as in Christ God forgave you." (Ephesians 4:32)

Do you want to be a GOOD person?
-- Spend time with God.
"Surely your goodness and love will follow me all the days of my life, and I will dwell in the house of the Lord forever." (Psalm 23:6)

Do you want to be FAITHFUL?
-- Spend time with God.
"The Lord, the Lord, the compassionate and gracious God, slow to anger, abounding in love and faithfulness." (Exodus 34:6)

Do you want to be a GENTLER person?
-- Spend time with God.
"Take my yoke upon you and learn from me, for I am gentle and humble in heart, and you will find rest for your souls." (Matthew 11:29)

Do you need more SELF-CONTROL?
-- Spend time with God.
"Rather, he must be hospitable, one who loves what is good, who is self-controlled, upright, holy and disciplined." (Titus 1:8)

As you spend time with God, connecting to the Core, the fruit of the Spirit will become evident in your own life. You will begin to exude love, joy, peace, patience, kindness, goodness, faithfulness, gentleness, and self-control. Only God can deliver all of that!

SPIRITUAL ENERGY
When you spend time with God, He restores you. Jesus said, "Come to me, all you who are weary and burdened, and I will give you rest." (Matthew 11:28) Do you need rest? Do you need energy?

Every living thing requires an energy source; something that gives it energy, power and helps it continue to live and thrive. Trees require water, sunlight, and carbon dioxide. Our physical bodies require food, water, and oxygen. But humans are more than just a physical body. We are also emotional and spiritual beings. While your emotional needs may be met by your friends and family, they are not equipped to meet your spiritual needs.

Even in the best-case scenario, with a great support system of friends and family around you, in the midst of major battles, you will find they are just not enough. It's not their fault; they are only human. You will need more help than people can give you.

You need to connect to a spiritual energy source. Like food and water is essential for your physical body, daily taking in energy from the Core is essential to maintain your spiritual strength. Warriors fuel their bodies with regular high-quality food, ensuring they are ready for battle. Spiritual warriors must do the same. We must maintain a Core connection, to daily be restored and renewed spiritually.

Take for example a video game. Have you ever played a game where your character needs to get powered up in order to fight? If you ignore the power level, your person gets slower, more sluggish, then your guard is weakened, while the enemy continues to attack. Eventually with no energy left, they fall to the ground in defeat. It's the same thing in our lives. If you neglect your spiritual fuel, you get weary, sluggish, the enemy attacks, and you will eventually fall in defeat if you don't replenish your power supply. If you had to gauge your spiritual energy level right now, what would it be?

LEVEL OF SPIRITUAL ENERGY

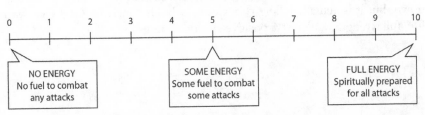

Most people go through their normal days in the lower levels. They don't have time, can't be bothered, they don't realize the importance, or have little interest in their spiritual energy level. All that changes when a crisis hits, someone gets sick, they lose their job, their friends or family relationships fall apart, etc. In those moments, they realize they need more spiritual energy, but many don't know how to get it. They don't know where the source is for the energy they need. Some turn to alcohol, drugs, or food. But substances that make our bodies feel good temporarily, do not provide spiritual energy.

Those who figure out their spiritual deficiency look for the Core, but in their desperate state, they are more susceptible to false religions, false teaching and deception. Those who are fortunate or had a good foundation of faith somewhere in their past, find their way back to the Core. They connect to the Core during the crisis, then go on their happy way once life is back to normal. Much like the foolish virgins in Matthew 25, they are foolishly unprepared for the next battle, and for judgment day...

Core connection is essential for spiritual energy and strength. If you hope to be victorious in the coming days, in life's spiritual battles, in fulfilling God's purpose for you, you must connect to the Core. When you connect to the Core, you receive from God your daily spiritual meal, your daily bread. Just as a person who only eats once a week will not be physically strong, a person who only has a spiritual meal once a week will not be spiritually strong.

We have options for what food we consume for physical energy, and we also have options for consuming spiritual energy. Some food is good for your body and some is bad for your body. Spiritual energy is the same. God, the Core, is the only energy source that is good for you, and will produce everlasting benefits for you. However, Satanism is clearly a very negative energy source that leads to death and destruction. The devil may also present himself in a positive spiritual manner. The Bible tells us, "Satan himself masquerades as an angel of light." (2 Corinthians 11:14)

Satan uses other religions or religious practices to draw people in. But what may appear good in the beginning is not actually good. Look to see, what are the fruit of that spiritual energy? Ultimately the same energy that presents itself as a good source for your healing is also the same source for your misery and torment. Think of it as junk food. It may taste good going down, but it is actually killing you. Conversely, the one true God gives you life, full strength, and 100% positive spiritual energy.

Chapter 14

MEET - RELEASE - RECEIVE

Within the Core connection three things occur: we meet with God, release to God, and receive from God. These occur within each element of Core connection: Word of God, Worship, and Prayer. The divine exchange that occurs when we meet with God is what feeds and restores our souls. This supernatural meeting accomplishes much more than we could work to achieve on our own.

MEET WITH GOD

INVITATION: In this meeting you are the host, and God, the King is your guest. You have invited the King, and He has graciously accepted the invitation. It is an honor to have the King of Kings come meet with you. Preparations must be made. You will want to honor the King's time and make Him feel welcome.

In any successful meeting, both parties are aware they are in a meeting, and generally have some type of advanced notification that a meeting will take place. An important meeting gets the priority on your schedule. It's never squeezed in if you have time. That's a sure way to never actually have a meeting! While it is true that God requires very little advanced warning, and His Spirit, that resides within us, is always accessible to us, planning to meet with God at a good time is generally more successful in maintaining a consistent Core connection.

LOCATION: When is the best time for you to meet with God? Each person's day is different, and most schedules are busy and can be erratic. When can you meet consistently? When can you meet to give your best to God? The meeting time and place should make it easy for you to give God your undivided attention. Are you an early bird or a night owl? When do you have a break in your day? When can you have time alone for your meeting? Pray and ask God to help you find the right time to meet.

What is the best place for you to meet with God? Do you like to be indoors or outdoors? Do you have a comfy chair, or a prayer closet? Where can you go to be alone with God? In order to hear His still small voice, a quiet place with few distractions is ideal. What adjustments will you need to make to accomplish this?

Every place has a feel to the atmosphere. Some places are peaceful, others feel instantly tense and stressful. Consider this when choosing your meeting place. The atmosphere needs to be inviting to the Spirit of God. If you share a home with unbelievers, find a small undisturbed area that you can spiritually cleanse before each meeting or consider another location.

TAKE ACTION

Work out the meeting details with God. He knows your schedule, your habits, your home, your atmosphere, and your distractions.

PRAY OUT LOUD

God please show me the best time and place to meet with you.
I want to honor You with our meeting.

Prepare to meet with the King.

RELEASE Burdens – RECEIVE Peace

Yes, you are meeting with the King, but He is also your Father. No matter what your earthly dad is like, God wants you to know and accept that He is a good, good Father. He loves you and wants to help you. With that in mind, He invites you to bring all your burdens to Him, "Come to me, all you who are weary and burdened, and I will give you rest. Take my yoke upon you and learn from me, for I am gentle and humble in heart, and you will find rest for your souls. For my yoke is easy and my burden is light." (Matthew 11:28-30)

God, your Father, invites you to release your burdens to Him. Let Him carry your heavy load. The load you were never made to carry. Your Father invites you to release the stress, the struggle, the worry over to Him. When you give your burdens to God, He is faithful to not just carry it, but to work it out for you.

Most burdens are beyond our control anyway, so why carry them? Give them to God. Jesus told us, "… with God all things are possible." (Matthew 19:26) You can trust God to do the impossible in your life and circumstances. The Bible tells us how to release burdens and receive peace, "Do not be anxious about anything, but in every situation, by prayer and petition, with thanksgiving, present your requests to God. And the peace of God, which transcends all understanding, will guard your hearts and your minds in Christ

Jesus." (Philippians 4:6-7) Once you pray and present your requests to God, that's when He pours out His peace that transcends all understanding.

You see, once you release your burden, you can receive God's peace. The peace of God transcends our reason. It doesn't make sense that you would have peace when your child is sick, but with God you can. It doesn't make sense that you would have peace when you just lost your job, but with God you can. When you release your burden to God, He will give you His peace. But, once you release your burden, leave it there! Don't pick it back up and carry it again. Sometimes you need to release, release, and release again, until the burden stays down! Then, you can keep your peace.

God is the Prince of Peace, so peace is important to God. (Isaiah 9:6) God told His priest to speak a blessing of peace over His people, "The Lord bless you and keep you; the Lord make his face shine on you and be gracious to you; the Lord turn his face toward you and give peace." (Numbers 6:24-26) God gives you the blessing of peace. Another blessing is, "May the God of hope fill you with all joy and peace as you trust in him, so that you may overflow with hope by the power of the Holy Spirit." (Romans 15:13)

Jesus also loved peace. He told his disciples, "Peace I leave with you; my peace I give you. I do not give to you as the world gives. Do not let your hearts be troubled and do not be afraid." (John 14:27) God gives us His peace. Take it, receive it and guard it. If you lose it, go back to God and get some more!

RELEASE Sin – RECEIVE Forgiveness

While you meet with God, you can also release sin. God has an amazing way of drawing our attention to sin and watching for us to respond. If you are willing to release it and repent of it quickly, that is better for you. As with releasing your burdens, releasing sin can sometimes be difficult. But, as we are told in Exodus, "Do not worship any other god, for the Lord, whose name is Jealous, is a jealous God." (Exodus 34:14) He will not allow His children to love their sin more than Him. If you choose to cling to your sin, and refuse to release it to God, it will become a wedge between you. It will hinder your relationship and ability to receive from God. Sin must be released and repented of quickly.

Whether you love your sin, or hate it, and think it is too big to be forgiven, you can release it to God. Jesus already paid the price for the forgiveness of your sins, "But he was wounded for our transgressions (sins); he was crushed for our iniquities (sins); upon him was the chastisement that brought us peace (he was hurt so we could have peace), and with his stripes we are healed (he was whipped, so we could be healed)." (Isaiah 53:5 author notes in parentheses) No sin is greater than the sacrifice Jesus made for you. He is able and willing to take all the sin you will release to Him. That's when healing can begin.

Once you release your sin, you can receive God's forgiveness. It's a beautiful exchange that can only happen with God. Only God is able to forgive us of our sins. God's forgiveness is complete, "as far as the east is from the west, so far has he removed our transgressions from us." (Psalm 103:12) God said, "For I will forgive their wickedness and will remember their sins no more." (Jeremiah 31:34) Jesus desires for you to release your sins and receive forgiveness.

RELEASE Forgiveness – RECEIVE Forgiveness

You can also release forgiveness. Part of the human experience is being hurt and hurting others. Even those with the best intentions and those who are most loving will inevitably experience hurting or being hurt. Just as hurting others requires repentance, being hurt requires forgiveness. You may be questioning the word, "requires." Yes, according to the word of God forgiveness is a requirement if we want our sins to be forgiven, "But if you do not forgive others their sins, your Father will not forgive your sins." (Matthew 6:15) Again, releasing forgiveness may not be easy, but it is necessary for you to receive forgiveness.

Once you begin to forgive others before God, He can begin the amazing work of forgiving and healing you. Yes, you can receive forgiveness and healing. But, holding onto unforgiveness blocks God's healing work on your heart and soul. When you meet with God, He can guide you through forgiving even the deepest hurts. The more you meet with Him, the more you will trust Him with this process.

* Forgiveness is a big topic that is covered in greater detail in Book 2: "Weapons & Armors, Prepared Warriors."

RELEASE Soul Wounds – RECEIVE Healing

You can also release pain, disappointment, hurts, and anger to God. When you release those things off of your soul and hand them to God, it allows Him to come in and heal you. Only God can heal the parts of us that are most in need of healing. Again, God will walk you through this process. He is the great physician. He knows how to remove those things that are deeply embedded, stuffed so far down no one else has access to them. But, God can. God will. God desires to take those things from you, repair, mend, and heal your soul.

One meeting with God can replace many counseling sessions. God can get to the root of the issue immediately because He knows your heart, He knows your history and He has seen everything. Things we can't see with our eyes are seen by God. He loves you and desires for you to be healed in mind, body, and soul.

Once you release your soul wounds, you can receive God's healing. A soul wound is like a wound that has been covered up, pushed a side, and is now festering with infection. God has an amazing way of bringing the wound to the surface again, removing the bandage, and flushing out the infection. He will completely clean the wound. This process can be painful, but trust God to complete the process. Once He has removed all the gunk, He will begin to heal your soul. If this is what you need, come meet with God. Let Him care for you.

RECEIVE FROM GOD

The beautiful part of each meeting with God is that you receive something. You will never leave the meeting empty handed. As you welcome God to the meeting, He also welcomes you. As you pour out love to God, He pours out His love for you. Anything you offer God; He turns around and doubles your offering right back to you.

A significant aspect of preparing to meet with God, is preparing yourself to receive all the love and goodness He will extend to you. For those who have never truly been loved, appreciated, or blessed this may be a difficult process. The part of your heart that receives may have been closed off. But trust that little by little God will break through and soften your heart to receive His love, forgiveness and healing.

THOSE WHO MEET WITH GOD

Throughout scriptures we see that God loves to meet with His people. He wants to be connected with us. He wants to have a relationship with us. If we come and meet with Him, we will see His great love, compassion and mercy for us. David loved to meet with God, "My soul thirsts for God, for the living God. When can I go and meet with God?" (Psalm 42:2) Perhaps that is why God called him, "a man after my own heart." (Acts 13:22)

Those who meet with God leave filled up and empowered. Scriptures say of the early church, "After they prayed, the place where they were meeting was shaken. And they were all filled with the Holy Spirit and spoke the word of God boldly." (Acts 4:31)

One of the most amazing examples in the Bible of meeting with God, is found in the book of Exodus. After God led the Israelites out of Egypt, He took time to meet with Moses. He met with Moses to guide and direct the people, and establish His laws and order here on earth. They met on top of Mount Sinai, "Mount Sinai was covered with smoke, because the Lord descended on it in fire. The smoke billowed up from it like smoke from a furnace, and the whole mountain trembled violently." (Exodus 19:18). Meeting with God, in all His amazing power and glory, will leave a lasting effect. Moses physically glowed, "When Moses came down from Mount Sinai with the two tablets of the covenant law in his hands, he was not aware that his face was radiant because he had spoken with the Lord." (Exodus 34:29) Spending time meeting with God can have amazing effects. Even as they traveled Moses set up a meeting place for the Lord,

> *Now Moses used to take a tent and pitch it outside the camp some distance away, calling it the "tent of meeting." Anyone inquiring of the Lord would go to the tent of meeting outside the camp. And whenever Moses went out to the tent, all the people rose and stood at the entrance to their tents, watching Moses until he entered the tent. As Moses went into the tent, the pillar of cloud would come down and stay at the entrance, while the Lord spoke with Moses. Whenever the people saw the pillar of cloud standing at the entrance to the tent, they all stood and worshiped, each at the entrance to their tent. The Lord would speak to Moses face to face, as one speaks to a friend. Then Moses would return to the camp, but his young aide Joshua son of Nun did not leave the tent. - Exodus 33:7-11*

What a beautiful picture of God's desire to meet with us. If you will establish a meeting place, and faithfully meet with God, what might you experience? When you meet with God His presence leaves a lasting effect. Moses experienced this, "When Moses came down from Mount Sinai with the two tablets of the covenant law in his hands, he was not aware that his face was radiant because he had spoken with the Lord." (Exodus 34:29) When you meet with God what lasting effect might you experience?

WORD - WORSHIP - PRAYER

There are three main elements for Core connection: The Word of God, Worship, and Prayer. When you meet with God, some days you may employ all three elements, two elements, or just one. But it is important to regularly engage in all three in order to have a well-rounded and fully connected relationship with God.

There is no legalistic format that must be followed. Some people like a structured time with God, and enjoy Bible reading plans. Others may enjoy more of a freeform to their meetings. Be open to God's leading and direction as you establish your time together. Some days you may be in the mood to worship most of the time, with small prayers and scripture accenting your worship.

Other days you may dive into the scriptures and feel hungry for more, as you ask the Holy Spirit to teach you. Or maybe you have a burden to pray over a situation in your life. Each day will present its own agenda. The important thing is that you are stopping to engage with God, enjoy His presence, and place yourself at His feet to worship and learn from the Master. Then, periodically take time to assess your meetings to ensure you are employing all three elements: The Word of God, Worship and Prayer.

CORE CONNECTION

Core connection is the awesome privilege of being invited to meet with God. Every time you meet with God, you are connecting to the Core, God. He is the source of everything you need. Just spending time with God will make you more like Him. Spending time with God will recharge your spiritual battery and nourish your soul. Find a time and place to meet with God. You will be rewarded for every moment of time you spend in His presence. As you release your burdens, hurts, sins and forgiveness, you will receive love, healing and forgiveness from God. This is an exchange that can only happen in the midst of a Core connection. Meeting regularly with God is essential for every Prepared Warrior to be spiritually prepared for life's battles and judgement day.

PART 4

WORD CONNECTION

Chapter 15

TJ'S STORY
THE LIVING WORD

Days moved on and life continued. TJ was doing his best to represent Christ at school, though it was more difficult now. He tried to catch up with Teyo and the other guys in his youth group as often as possible. It really helped to remember he was not alone. There were others who were on the same journey. He loved his mom, but their relationship seemed really strained lately, and he didn't know why. Then there was the problem with lust. He didn't intend to keep falling into the same trap. But it always seemed to pop up when he was already weak, and then it was harder to resist.

TJ's angel, Nigel, held his position. He was aware of the attacks the enemy was carrying out against TJ, but TJ seemed to have no idea he was under attack. TJ also had no idea that armor and weapons were available to him. TJ had so much to learn. Nigel was anxious to see TJ grow and learn about God, and all the power that is accessible to him. As he learned to call on God, Nigel's gifts would be called into use. Soon. Very soon TJ would learn.

For now, Nigel stood resolute. He held the wisdom of the ages, knowing each person must face temptation, each person must learn to turn from sin and turn to God. He would not be ruffled or discouraged. Nigel's mission was clear; he was there as TJ's guardian, and to do what God commanded. His first mission is to reveal tools to TJ that will help him grow closer to God. The angel had carefully prepared to introduce TJ to the, "sword of the Spirit, which is the word of God." (Ephesians 6:17) It is the double-edged sword that God said, "goes out from my mouth: It will not return to me empty, but will accomplish what I desire and achieve the purpose for which I sent it." (Isaiah 55:11) The sword, the Word is essential for every warrior and the angel was instructed to get it into TJ's hands as soon as possible.

It was Sunday morning, and TJ was now in the habit of attending church every Sunday. As he arrived, Nigel caught a glimpse of a fellow messenger angel departing the church, having just delivered his message. Ah, the plan was coming together perfectly. Now, if the Pastor would only hear and obey the message the angel delivered.

As the service started, and everyone found their way to the sanctuary, TJ spotted Teyo and the other kids in the youth group. They claimed their usual spot at the front on the left side of the sanctuary. They all found their seats, carrying their Bibles in various colors. TJ had never noticed that before. But, yes, every one of his friends and classmates had their Bibles with them. TJ looked down at his empty hands. He made a mental note to find a Bible he could bring next week.

As the congregation worshiped TJ's angel was keeping a close eye on the Pastor, who seemed to be in deep thought. His serious face was earnest and focused. The angel sent up a prayer, "God help him to hear and obey your words." Then, his attention shifted back to TJ. He delighted in seeing TJ worship God. How grateful he was to serve under this young man. His heart surely delighted the Lord.

As the worship drew to a close, the Pastor knew that was his cue to take the stage and begin the message. The Pastor hesitated, and the band leader smoothly continued the music for a bit longer, giving him a chance to gather his thoughts and take the stage. The congregation seemed to notice the pause in service, and heads turned to see what was going on.

However, Nigel's attention was drawn to a dear intercessor on the side of the sanctuary, she began to pray. Her sweet prayers were well known in heaven. Her great love for the Lord garnered great excitement amongst the angels, who loved to be near such adoration for the King. Nigel whispered, "Yes, dear sister, pray and ask God to strengthen your Pastor. He needs the Holy Spirit to strengthen and speak through him today." Nigel wondered if she heard him, as her eyes turned to the Pastor, and her prayer focus zeroed in on her target.

The Pastor breathed deep, and shook his head in agreement, as if to answer an unspoken question. As the Pastor stood and made his way to the stage, the band leader expertly tapered the music to hand the stage over to the Pastor. With a deep breath, the Pastor began, "Good morning church. I will not be delivering my prepared message today. I believe God has different plans, and I want to be obedient to His agenda, not mine."

For the next hour, the Pastor went on to share his testimony, one the church had never heard. He told of his difficult childhood. How he felt abandoned and forgotten. He told of the trials he had endured. Most of them heart wrenching. There was not a dry eye in the room.

By the time he turned the corner to tell of how God's great love overwhelmed him, just when he was about to lose all hope, a collective cheer rose from the congregation. God had not left him. God had not forgotten him. God did see him, and God did love him. The great joy of being called into a family, God's family, was so overwhelming that it changed his life forever.

The Pastor closed his message with one last note, "Life can be difficult, even after you know Christ. But I want to share with you something that has helped me through some very rough times." Then, he pulled out a little note card from his wallet, "I carry this with me all the time. I pull it out every time I get overwhelmed or discouraged. It reads, 'God is my refuge and strength, an ever-present help in trouble.' I personalized Psalm 46:1." With that the Pastor closed in prayer.

The dear intercessor delighted in every detail of the Pastor's story. She knew God so well she didn't doubt for a moment his goodness or how the story would go. With her hands clasped over her heart, she turned her smiling face toward heaven. She thought to herself, that's just like God to save this young man, that's why she loves her Savior so.

With his job done, the Pastor took his seat, while the musicians took the stage once more. He took another deep breath of relief this time. He had no idea how hard it would be to revisit some of those memories, and to speak them out loud. But at the same time, he had no idea the feeling of relief it would bring. With every memory he unloaded, another weight lifted from his shoulders. He felt lighter and lighter.

God opened his eyes, even while he was speaking, to the depth of His love for him. How God had truly carried him through so many trials. He could now see so clearly how powerful the Word of God was, though it was tattered and worn, folded in his pocket. He whispered a prayer of thanks to the Lord. God had something going on this morning. He could only pray that God's will was done through the sharing of his story. The Pastor was thankful he chose to obey the Lord. He had done his part.

TJ sat stunned. He had no idea his Pastor had endured such hardship, pain, and rejection. The shadow of his old self was nowhere to be seen. He is a completely new person, healed, restored, renewed. Then, when TJ heard the Pastor share the scripture from his notecard, the words seemed to magnify in his ears.

TJ had no idea what just happened, but the scripture hit somewhere deep inside of him. It was just what he was looking for. He needed refuge and strength. He wanted an ever-present help. Maybe he would make himself a notecard with that very same scripture. He jotted a quick note, to remind himself.

> *God is my refuge and strength, an ever-present help in trouble.*
> *- Psalm 46:1 personalized*

TJ's angel, Nigel, delighted to see the Word spring forth from the Pastor's mouth, as a double edge sword. The sword went straight to TJ's heart, slicing it with greater precision than the most gifted surgeon. It cut off a hard piece of stone. Then bright gold glowing Words were sewn, as thread, into TJ's heart. The Word miraculously turned TJ's heart to brand new healthy flesh.

Nigel peered at the paper in TJ's hand. Yes, the Pastor's message had hit its mark. He smiled to himself. Wasn't it just like God to accomplish so many wonderful things, all in one person's act of obedience? The Pastor, the intercessor and TJ were all blessed, along with so many more in the congregation. As each believer heard the testimony of God's goodness, the Holy Spirit within them grew bigger and shined brighter. Nigel would never grow tired of watching the Holy Spirit work and move.

TJ was now in possession of something so powerful. He didn't know the power yet, but he would soon learn that the Word of God was more powerful than any enemy he would face. If this one verse could strengthen, encourage, and empower him, imagine what the entire Word of God could do in his life! This was just the beginning!

Chapter 16

WORD CONNECTION

How do you get to know someone? Choose someone you admire. Maybe that someone is famous, a celebrity, athlete, or a government leader? It would be such an honor to meet them and get to know them one-on-one. But, because they are famous, it is highly unlikely that you will actually get a meeting, and if you did it would likely be very brief.

The next best option would be to read their autobiography. When you read their autobiography, you learn about them as they explain their life, and their thoughts, in their own words. Your next step may be to look for a reputable biography. Then, you can learn about them from other people who know them well or have studied them extensively.

Or, you may read the tabloids, or follow the gossip columns. Maybe you even listen to people who are fans of the famous person, but have never met them, or spent any time with them. The information they provide about them may not be correct, as their love and devotion for the famous person may overtake the truth. In their attempt to encourage others to love them, they may try to explain away anything deemed undesirable, or flawed in the famous person's decisions, actions or words. To make them universally appealing, the truth may get in the way.

The most reliable method of knowing someone is to connect with them directly and consistently. It is the same with God. It is not enough to read books about Him, hear others talk about Him, watch videos about Him, or imagine you know Him. To truly know God, you must read His Word.

The Word of God is a consistent and reliable way we can hear God's voice here on earth. If you want to know God, you must read His Word. The Bible says, "In the beginning was the Word, and the Word was with God, and the Word was God." (John 1:1) God is inexplicably connected to His Word. There is no better way to find out who God is, how He works, what He thinks, and what He requires from us, than to read His Word.

The Bible is God's letter to us. We know, "All Scripture is God-breathed and is useful for teaching, rebuking, correcting and training in righteousness, so that the servant of God may be thoroughly equipped for every good work." (2 Timothy 3:16-17) Every Word in the Bible is useful and important. It is unwise to only keep your favorite Words and discard the rest. To fully know God, you must fully know His Word, all of His Words.

Our goal with this book is to help you make a true Core connection with God. **The first and most essential method for Core connection is reading the Word of God.** Yes, worship and prayer are also powerful ways to connect with God, but reading the Word is even more important than worship. Reading the Word is even more important than prayer. Why? Because when you study God's Word, you are committed to learn and understand who God really is. When you read the Word of God on a regular basis, you continue to take in the truth about God and His character. The more you know the truth about God, the less likely you will be deceived or believe a lie.

It is easy to believe a lie about God. The devil, the father of lies, is actively at work attempting to dilute, and mislead people about who God really is. We saw that clearly with Adam and Eve in the beginning. The serpent, the devil, caused Adam and Eve to question God, and that led to sin (Genesis 3). Part of our own sinful nature is to create a god in our own image, one that is pleasing to us. This god doesn't challenge us to conform to it, rather it conforms to our wishes.

Many people make up their own gods in their minds. They pray to their god; they worship their god. But their god is not the one true God. They have just created an idol to worship and called it god. To avoid the mistake and sin of idolatry, it is essential to read the Word of God, to know who God really is. Then, your prayers and worship will be aligned with, directed to, and connect you with the one true God.

Chapter 17

WORD
MEET - RELEASE - RECEIVE

Any scholar can read the Word of God from an educational standpoint. People from other religions read the Word of God, to learn about Christianity. Not everyone who reads the Bible is meeting with God. Jesus told some Jewish leaders, "You study the scriptures diligently because you think that in them you have eternal life. These are the very Scriptures that testify about me, yet you refuse to come to me to have life." (John 5:39) The scriptures are not just words to read and laws to follow, they tell of God himself.

For Prepared Warriors, the first goal we have when reading the Word of God is to meet with God. God, Jesus, is the Word, "The Word became flesh and made his dwelling among us. We have seen his glory, the glory of the one and only Son, who came from the Father, full of grace and truth." (John 1:14) Again, Jesus is described as, "...dressed in a robe dipped in blood, and his name is the Word of God." (Revelation 19:13) So, at the end of the day, if you didn't meet Jesus while reading the Word of God, you missed the point.

How you position yourself and prepare your mind when you read the Word of God will make a difference in how you receive it. When you come to meet with God, and open His Word, you should come expecting to meet with God, and expecting His Word to come alive to teach and instruct you. Jesus told his disciples, "... The words I have spoken to you – they are full of Spirit and life." (John 6:63) As you read the Word realize it is full of Spirit and life. Reach out and receive the full measure of the Word of God.

Take hold of the Word as a gift, something to be treasured in your heart. Among the wisdom found in the book of Proverbs, it reads, "My son, pay attention to what I say; turn your ear to my words. Do not let them out of your sight, keep them within your heart." (Proverbs 4:20-21) When you meet with God to read His word, come in with a heart ready to receive a precious gift.

Remember your meeting includes an "Invitation" and "Location." Your invitation may be a simple prayer like, "Holy Spirit I invite you to be my teacher today. Come breathe life into your Word. You are invited to realign me, correct me, and teach me. Help me know you better." Every time you come to meet with God, He has an agenda. God is constantly at work in your life. Once He knows you plan to meet with Him, He will begin taking you on the journey of getting to know Him, getting to know yourself, and all He created you to be and do.

Your location may change but is always important to find a time and place that allows you to focus, and truly read or hear the Word of God. For the purposes of Core connection, taking in God's Word while meeting with the King, will be different from scripture memorization, devotional reading, or even studying to teach the Word. All of those things are good and worthy, but different than reading the Word to meet with and receive from God.

RELEASE

As you meet with God, He will help you release and receive. It is your time to release your burdens, worries, stress, anxiety, sin, rebellion, and misunderstandings about who God is. Then you are ready to receive love, hope, joy, peace, goodness, light, healing, and the truth about God. This is a regular cleansing process that is important for your spiritual health, which affects your mental and physical health too. All of this can be accomplished by reading the Word being open and aware that God will speak to you through His word.

God is able to separate within us our own ways, from His ways, "For the word of God is alive and active. Sharper than any double-edged sword, it penetrates even to dividing soul and spirit, joints and marrow; it judges the thoughts and attitudes of the heart." (Hebrews 4:12) As we take in the Word of God, He makes our thoughts and attitudes clear. We begin to see ourselves through His eyes. We begin to understand His holiness. We begin to understand His ways.

There are two warnings we need to address here. The first is for those who are afraid or unwilling to read God's Word because they know it will convict them of sin. While it is true that God's Word brings conviction and makes us feel uncomfortable in sin, that is a good thing. Your discomfort should lead you to repent, "Godly sorrow brings repentance that leads to salvation and leaves no regret, but worldly sorry brings death." (2 Corinthians 7:10)

Don't be afraid to read God's Word. God is not a task master, or grumpy teacher, who requires you to complete set tasks. He does not pound you on the head, condemning you for your sins. You are not getting called to the principal's office or in trouble each time you meet with God. No, you will see, as you read His Word, God is, "... the compassionate and gracious God, slow to anger, abounding in love and faithfulness, maintaining love to thousands, and forgiving wickedness, rebellion and sin. Yet he does not leave the guilty unpunished..." (Exodus 34:6-7) Those are God's own words about Himself! So, if you are fearful of reading God's Word because of your sin, and don't want to feel even worse about yourself, let's put your mind at ease.

> *... God's kindness is intended to lead you to repentance.*
> *- Romans 2:4*

The process of God correcting us when we sin was never meant to be harsh or particularly painful. We have a tendency to make it harder by taking longer and holding onto sin instead of humbly repenting. If we make a point of quickly repenting whenever we sin, it is better for us. The Bible says, "Whoever conceals their sin does not prosper, but the one who confesses and renounces them finds mercy." (Proverbs 28:13) Confessing sin is part of the releasing process. Once you confess sin to God, you can receive His grace and mercy.

God longs to show you grace and compassion when you confess your sins. Isaiah wrote, "Yet the Lord longs to be gracious to you; therefore, he will rise up to show you compassion. For the Lord is a God of justice. Blessed are all who wait for him!" (Isaiah 30:18) Trying to ignore or hide sin when you meet with God doesn't work. He sees all and knows all. It only hurts you and hinders your relationship with God when you refuse to repent of sin.

God is not like a self-righteous man, who shakes his finger at you, and shames you. God is not like Satan, who condemns and accuses you. There is a huge difference between shame, condemnation, and accusations and the Holy Spirit's conviction over sin. Shame, condemnation and accusations are all meant to keep you bound and imprisoned by sin. Satan would love to discredit you and make you feel unworthy and separate you from God.

But, the Holy Spirit convicts you of sin, so that you will turn from it, and turn to God. In this way you will receive forgiveness and freedom from sin. God has a special way of using His Word to shine the light on the sin in your life, even sin you may not have even seen before. Once you see it and are convicted (uncomfortable), you can repent and turn from it. God is waiting for you to release sin, then He can step in and heal that part of your soul.

You are not the first, and you will not be the last to sin. Here it is again, just so you remember, "for all have sinned and fall short of the glory of God." (Romans 3:23) God knew this would be our condition. We cannot be as holy and righteous as God. The best we can do is regularly repent and believe that Jesus's blood paid the price for our forgiveness.

The second warning came from the Apostle, James. Reading the Word is not enough; we must also do what it says. Obeying God and His Word reaps many blessings. You are deceived if you think you can continue to sin and have a relationship with God. James said, "Therefore, get rid of all moral filth and the evil that is so prevalent and humbly accept the word planted in you, which can save you. Do not merely listen to the word, and so deceive yourselves. Do what it says." (James 1:21-22) If you humble yourself to accept the Word, and do what it says, you will rid yourself of sin.

There is wisdom in doing what the Word says, "Therefore everyone who hears these words of mine and puts them into practice is like a wise man who built his house on the rock." (Matthew 7:24) There are also blessings for those who obey the Word, "Blessed rather are those who hear the word of God and obey it." (Luke 11:28) As you read the Word and do what it says, blessings will begin to unfold in your life.

As this process happens, in your quest to be more like Christ, you begin to release, repent, and align with God. This is a wonderful, freeing, healing process. God knows you. He knows you better than you know yourself. He has a plan, specifically for you, to take you through this process in such a way that you will be willing to release sin, and anything that separates you from the one who loves you so much. As you willingly release the old you, you open yourself up to receive the new you from God.

RECEIVE

Every day, every moment your soul is receiving something. Your eyes and ears are gateways to your soul. Whatever you watch, you take in and receive. Whatever you hear you take in and receive. The more you watch or listen to something, the more like it you become.

There is a negative side to that. If you watch the news all the time, you become stressed, fearful, angry, or divided. If you watch pornography all the time, you become obsessed with sex. You get the picture. But there is also a good side to this. If you view nature all the time, you may have more peace and tranquility. Most importantly, if you read or hear God's Word all the time, you become more like God.

What do you watch or listen to daily? Is it making you better or worse? When you receive the Word of God blessings and benefits are so abundant, you may wonder why everyone isn't reading this book? Good question! There is no possible way to measure the fullness of what you will receive from the Word. But we do know there are many blessings you can receive.

The first and most important blessing of reading God's Word is that you get to meet with God. Is there any higher privilege and honor than meeting with God? Is there any higher wisdom or authority than God? And yet, He is willing to meet with us every time we invite Him, every time we open His Word. It's amazing.

FEAR OF THE LORD

Many people, even Christians, place God on the back shelf in their lives. Something to be handled later, when they have time. But when you read God's Word you receive a healthy fear of the Lord. It is a regular reminder that there is a God, He is above us, He sees and knows all, and we will all have to answer to Him one day for everything we have ever said, done, or thought. Jesus said, "Do not be afraid of those who kill the body but cannot kill the soul. Rather, be afraid of the One who can destroy both soul and body in hell." (Matthew 10:28) If that doesn't put the fear of God in you, then I don't know what will!

It is important to hear God's Word so we can obey it. But even those who have not heard God's Word will still be accountable for it on judgment day. So, remaining ignorant of the law doesn't save you from it.

Regularly reading God's Word helps us remember, and places before us a constant awareness of the accountability for our sin, which is a good thing. Moses commanded the priests, "… you shall read this law before them in their hearing. Assemble the people—men, women and children, and the foreigners residing in your towns—so they can listen and learn to fear the Lord your God and follow carefully all the words of this law. Their children, who do not know this law, must hear it and learn to fear the Lord your God as long as you live in the land you are crossing the Jordan to possess." (Deuteronomy 31:11-13) Moses knew it was important to read the Word of God, so the people would not stray from His commands, especially as they were entering a land filled with very sinful people.

Before Moses died, he spoke to the Israelites saying, "…Take to heart all the words I have solemnly declared to you this day, so that you may command your children to obey carefully all the words of this law. They are not just idle words for you – they are your life. By them you will live long in the land you are crossing the Jordan to possess." (Deuteronomy 32:46-47) Moses truly understood the importance of knowing and remembering God's Word. Fearing God would keep the people from falling into all kinds of sin. He declares that the Words, "are your life." So, receive the gift of life found in the Word of God.

There is a great story about King Josiah in 2 Chronicles 34. Since becoming King, he had already begun to cleanse the kingdom of all the false gods and idols. Then, he gave the order for the temple of God to be repaired. In the midst of the repairs Hilkiah, the priest, found the book of the law. The King's response to hearing the Word of God was dramatic, "When the king heard the words of the Law, he tore his robes. He gave these orders to Hilkiah, Ahikam son of Shaphan, Abdon son of Micah, Shaphan the secretary and Asaiah the king's attendant: 'Go and inquire of the LORD for me and for the remnant in Israel and Judah about what is written in this book that has been found. Great is the LORD's anger that is poured out on us because those who have gone before us have not kept the word of the LORD; they have not acted in accordance with all that is written in this book.'" (2 Chronicles 34:18-21) King Josiah had great respect, honor, and fear of the Lord, which was magnified when He heard the Word of the Lord for himself.

It is a great gift that we can hear God's Word for ourselves. Do you know what God commands? Do you know His laws? It's time to read God's Word and find out!

PRICELESS

One of the most moving things to behold is a Christian receiving a Bible for the first time. There was a village of Christians in a remote part of the world. They learned of Christ through missionaries but did not have a Bible in their own language. After years of waiting, the Bible was finally translated and delivered to the village. When the boxes were opened the villagers rushed in to get their own Bible. Tears streamed down their faces as they held their Bibles high, kissing them, and hugging them tightly to their chests. In most parts of the world we take for granted our access to such a treasured possession. It is good to be reminded.

When you read God's Word you receive a priceless treasure. For those wise enough to drink deeply of God's word, they emerge with the understanding of how amazing and priceless it is. There are few more vocal in adoration than David. The entire chapter of Psalm 119 David sings the praise of the Word of God. David lovingly wrote, "The law from your mouth is more precious to me than thousands of pieces of silver and gold." (Psalm 119:72) He also said, "And the words of the LORD are flawless, like silver purified in a crucible, like gold refined seven times. (Psalm 12:6) The Word of God is a most treasured possession, something to be held with honor, respect and love.

How do you see God's Word? Do you cherish it and regard it as more priceless than silver and God? It's time to read God's Word and discover the riches!

POWERFUL

When you read God's Word you will understand it is powerful! We see in Genesis, "And God said, 'Let there be light,' and there was light." (Genesis 1:1) God's Words are so powerful, He simply speaks things into existence. He created the entire world with just his Words.

> **By the word of the LORD the heavens were made,**
> **their starry host by the breath of his mouth.**

> *He gathers the waters of the sea into jars;*
> *he puts the deep into storehouses.*
> *Let all the earth fear the LORD;*
> *let all the people of the world revere him.*
> *For he spoke, and it came to be;*
> *he commanded, and it stood firm.*
> *- Psalm 33:4-9*

God's word creates. God's word goes out and accomplishes all He intends it to accomplish. Even the angels testify, "For no word from God will ever fail." (Luke 1:37) God's words aren't empty promises. They are backed by His supreme authority. God reminds us:

> *"For my thoughts are not your thoughts,*
> *neither are your ways my ways,"*
> *declares the LORD.*
> *"As the heavens are higher than the earth,*
> *so are my ways higher than your ways*
> *and my thoughts than your thoughts.*
> *As the rain and the snow*
> *come down from heaven,*
> *and do not return to it*
> *without watering the earth*
> *and making it bud and flourish,*
> *so that it yields seed for the sower and bread for the eater,*
> *so is my word that goes out from my mouth:*
> *It will not return to me empty,*
> *but will accomplish what I desire*
> *and achieve the purpose for which I sent it."*
> *- Isaiah 55:8-12*

What might God's word accomplish in your life. What powerful words has God spoken over you? It's time to read God's Word and find out!

GUIDE

When you read God's Word you receive guidance. Those who love God want to do His will. How can you know if you are on the right path? Read God's Word, and you will find the path, "Your word is a lamp for my feet, a light on my path." (Psalm 119:105) God lights the way for us through His Word, "The unfolding of your words gives light; it gives understanding to the simple."

(Psalm 119:130) God's Word is so amazing that even a child, or the simple can understand and be guided by it.

When you find yourself in a time of transition, or stepping out into the unknown, God's Word is a sure guiding light. Joshua's message to the Israelites, as they transitioned into the Kingdom God prepared for them, directed them to God's Word, "Be strong and very courageous. Be careful to obey all the law my servant Moses gave you; do not turn from it to the right or to the left, that you may be successful wherever you go. Keep this Book of the Law always on your lips; meditate on it day and night, so that you may be careful to do everything written in it. Then you will be prosperous and successful." (Joshua 1:7-8) The message is true for all times, and for all mankind; read the Word, do what it says, and you will be successful.

No matter what problem you face, or obstacles come your way, you can find guidance in the Word of God. Yes, we live in a different time than when the Bible was written, but as wise King Solomon wrote, "What has been will be again, what has been done will be done again; there is nothing new under the sun." (Ecclesiastes 1:9) You may think you have all new problems, and the Bible is too outdated to have any answers. Boy, are you in for a surprise? Ask God to guide you as you read His Word. He will bring you to passages you may have read before, but now they speak directly to you in your situation. When you read God's Word you will receive guidance.

What problems do you face today? Have you gone to God's Word to find guidance? It's time to read God's Word and let Him guide you.

DAILY BREAD

In the Core connection section, we talked about Spiritual Energy and how important it is to connect to God daily to sustain you. Well, in the Bible that concept has a name; it is called your "daily bread." Much like your physical body needs daily bread, your spiritual self also needs daily bread. So, where do you get this spiritual daily bread? I'm glad you asked!

When you read God's Word you receive your daily bread. The idea of receiving your daily bread began with the Israelites. When they left Egypt to cross the desert to the Promised Land, who literally dropped bread, manna, from the sky for them to eat each day. Thus, God gave them their daily bread. Moses told them, "He humbled you, causing you to hunger and then feeding you with manna, which neither you nor your ancestors had known, to teach you that man does not live on bread alone but on every word that comes from the mouth of the Lord. (Deuteronomy 8:3) So, the Word of the Lord becomes our daily bread. We humbly require God to give us His word each day to sustain us.

Jesus said, "It is written: 'Man shall not live on bread alone, but on every word that comes from the mouth of God.'" (Matthew 4:4) Jesus then taught his disciples to pray, what we now know as "The Lord's Prayer." Part of this prayer is asking God to, "give us today our daily bread." (Matthew 6:11) Now, God, in His wisdom and power, may be combining a request for daily physical and spiritual food. We need both!

Over and over in scripture we see the Word of God being compared to bread, because just as bread sustains our physical bodies, the Word of God sustains our Spiritual bodies. Are you receiving your daily bread? How spiritually hungry are you? It's time to read God's Word and receive your daily bread.

FAITH, HOPE, PEACE

When you read God's Word you receive faith, hope, and peace. You don't have to worry about the world anymore because you realize God is in control. You don't have to lose hope because you know the end of the story, and God wins! You can have peace in the midst of the storm, because you know God loves you and will take care of you, even when everything seems like a mess. God's word gives you perspective, God's perspective. From where He sits, there is no worry or fear. The more we read the Word of God, the more we will have God's perspective on our own lives, and the world around us.

Reading the Word of God will build your faith. It is written, "Consequently, faith comes from hearing the message, and the message is heard through the word about Christ." (Romans 10:17) As you read God's Word and see all that He has done in the past, it doesn't make your circumstances seem so impossible. In fact, you realize that, "With man this is impossible, but with God all things are possible." (Matthew 19:26)

It's easy to lose hope when you watch the news or read the papers. But, when you read the Word of God, it restores your hope. King David said, "You are my refuge and my shield; I have put my hope in your word," and "I wait for the Lord, my whole being waits, and in his word, I put my hope." (Psalm 119:114 and 130:5) He didn't put his hope in his family, his kingdom, or even his army. King David put his hope in God's Word, which is eternal, never changing.

To attain the peace of God in this present age is an elusive quest. But, again, King David gives us a great clue of where to find it. He said, "Great peace have those who love your law, and nothing can make them stumble." (Psalm 119:165) When you love the Word and laws of the Lord, you have peace. When you are in alignment and agreement with God's word, your soul can have peace.

Those who reject God and His Word, are the ones who are in a constant state of unrest and distress. Even if nothing else is going your way, just knowing you are right with God, will give you great peace. Because we know, "… If God is for us, who can be against us?" (Romans 8:31) So, take heart. Let the Word of God grow your faith, give you hope and peace. It's time to read God's Word.

ETERNAL TRUTH

As the world around us changes daily, and the social expectations become more absurd, it is reassuring to know that God's Word is eternal. When you read God's Word you receive eternal truth. Jesus said, "… If you hold to my teaching, you are really my disciples. Then you will know the truth, and the truth will set you free." (John 8:31-32)

There is freedom in knowing for sure what the truth is. You don't have to guess day after day how to act to please God, "Jesus Christ is the same yesterday and today and forever." (Hebrews 13:8) You don't have to search for the latest wisdom or hear each person's truth. Jesus already told us, "I am the way and the truth and the life. No one comes to the Father except through me." (John 14:6) So, Jesus, the Word, is the truth, and the truth is also eternal.

Truth is not subjective. Opinions are subjective, but truth is a solid immovable reality. It doesn't change with times, seasons or opinions. The truth is a solid foundation. The Word of God is truth and a solid foundation for building your life.

We know, "Your word, LORD, is eternal; it stands firm in the heavens." (Psalm 119:89) The Word of God is eternal, not just here on earth, but in the heavens. Beyond that, Jesus said, "Heaven and earth will pass away, but my words will never pass away." (Matthew 24:35) Are you getting the picture? God's Word is greater than time or location. It cannot be contained or outlasted. Are you looking for the truth? It's time to read God's Word and receive eternal truth.

WORD CONNECTION

The first and most essential method for Core connection is reading the Word of God. You can't skip over it and truly connect to God. It's too easy for us to fall into idolatry and create our own god to fit our liking. Reading the Word of God reveals God as He truly is. That's the only way to have a true relationship with Him. When you meet with God to read His Word a sacred exchange happens. You begin to release all of the burdens, sin, and brokenness that has held you back. Then, you are able to receive the goodness of God to forgive and heal you from the inside out. The Word of God is truly transformative. It's time to read God's Word.

TAKE ACTION

Today is a great day to start reading the Word of God. There is no need to wait for the perfect time, or the perfect place, or the perfect circumstances.

Start now! There will always be a reason why you can't. Let's talk about how you can.

- Read a chapter first thing in the morning
- Listen to the audio Bible on your way to work or school
- Listen to the audio Bible over lunch break
- Read a chapter for yourself or to your kids before bed
- Most Bible apps include the option to listen to the audio Bible
- Listening and reading at the same time increases comprehension

Just get started. You can refine the process later.

NOTE: The devil will try to come against you when you start to read the Word of God. Be prepared to withstand his attacks, of discouragement, busyness, etc. Plan now to NEVER GIVE UP!

As for God, his way is perfect; The Lord's word is flawless;
he shields all who take refuge in him. - 2 Samuel 22:31

THE CORE

PART 5

WORSHIP CONNECTION

Chapter 18

TJ'S STORY
TRUE WORSHIP

TJ proved to be a bigger problem than the demons anticipated. What started with one pesky scripture turned into a fascination with the Word of God. He was a sponge for learning and seemed to want to know more and more about God. He took steps to find good teachers and read everything he could get his hands on.

However, the demon's screen plan had slowed TJ down considerably. He could no longer focus on God when he got online. Suggestive pictures popped up almost immediately. Every ad on the side of the screens also displayed tempting images and text. The demons had seen to that! Their vast network of demons held control over so many humans. They worked like a well-oiled machine, pumping more and more sinful content onto the world wide web daily.

TJ was struggling. He knew he was, but it was too embarrassing to talk to anyone about it. He should be stronger than that. He should be able to just resist temptation and get to where he was going online. But the images made it difficult to turn away, or to even remember what he came online to do. For a while he continued to go online, determined to get past it, and continue his study. But it was just more and more difficult.

Then, he decided to just focus on finding good books, that would keep him off his phone, and he could still learn. Books were good, there were a lot of great authors and scholars who shared a lot of wisdom through their books. But, a lot of the world is online now. He couldn't even complete his schoolwork without getting online. This presented a problem for TJ, and not one he was able to tackle on his own.

The demons chuckled. Every time they caught TJ in their trap, his angel would turn away, unwilling to witness the vulgar display. The demons would taunt and laugh from a distance, "Ha, ha, ha! You thought we couldn't get to TJ with you here. We told you he would come back. We told you we would get to him. He's ours. He will always be ours!"

It was Sunday morning and TJ woke up to his alarm. But the grimace in his spirit, took his usual excitement, and caused TJ to linger in bed. The demons watched with anticipation. It always delighted them when a well laid trap continued to unwind even after their job was complete. All they had to do was trap them in some type of sin, then the human, feeling guilt and shame, separates themselves from God! Ha, ha!!

Sure, a well-placed comment of condemnation was always a good insurance policy, but they had found that humans are experts at condemning themselves. Guilt and shame are two wonderfully useful tools for separating people from God. As long as they feel unworthy, unlovable, unforgivable, they would maintain their distance from God, from church, from any believer who carried the Holy Spirit. It would just be too hard for them to be near any holiness.

Nigel was unmoved by their taunting. TJ was still so new to the faith. He had so much to learn. Of course, the demons could trip him up now. But he would grow and learn in time. Nigel was already focused on his next mission. He was instructed to introduce something so beautiful and simple it is often overlooked and under-utilized. But yielded correctly, it is extremely powerful. Nigel would help guide TJ to connect directly to God through worship.

The Lord saw to it that extra angels arrived for the worship service this morning. Glorious angels gifted in worship, flooded into the sanctuary. Nigel was delighted to see the Worship Pastor in the little back room kneeling in prayer before the service even started. She was crying out to God and petitioning on behalf of the church. She was calling on the Holy Spirit to meet with them and move in a real way for every person who entered the building. The Holy Spirit hovered near her as she prayed, listening intently, and glowing with excitement and agreement with her requests. Yes, God loves to come where He is invited and exalted.

In spite of the way he was feeling, TJ got up and willed himself to church. He was thankful he had made some friends. They always made him feel welcome, even when he was feeling down. The worship music started, and TJ began to sing along. He generally sings quietly, because he's not a very good singer. But today the music was loud enough, and everyone around him was singing out, so he thought, "Why not?". When he broke out of his worship box, and started to sing louder, it felt so good. He felt bold and free.

TJ's angel, Nigel, watched as TJ worshiped and the air around him filled with streams of color, flowing from him. One small beam of white light came from his mouth, as his voice. But flooding the area all around him were beams and streams of every color. Each stream holding the truth, love, and joy emitted while pure worship was released from TJ's soul to his Creator.

In the midst of worship TJ could feel the love of God come down and wrap around him like a warm blanket. With such great love surrounding Him, TJ dropped to his knees, "God I love you. I want to please you. I repent of all of my sins. I don't want to sin against you, but I am having such a hard time stopping."

The Lord's heart was moved by TJ's humble prayer of repentance. Instantly, an angel was dispatched to collect the precious prayer, a poof of sweet-smelling incense, and bring it before the throne of God. Forgiveness flooded from the throne, Jesus delighted in the exchange, seeing his blood begin to cover the black spot that was within TJ's heart. It was no more.

Still kneeling in the warmth of God's love, TJ instantly felt relief. He had no idea just being honest with God would feel so good. Why had he waited? Did he think God would reject him, or stop loving him when he messed up? God's response was so immediate, and so full of love, grace, and mercy. Gratitude overwhelmed TJ, "Thank you God. Thank you for hearing my cry. Thank you for forgiving me. Thank you for still loving me." TJ's angel stood as a witness to the beautiful exchange and couldn't help but lift up praise to God as well, "Father you are full of grace and mercy. Praise be to God!"

TJ was now introduced to the amazing wonder of connecting with God through worship. He truly communed and communicated with God in the midst of worship. It's like God was right there with him. TJ would never look at worship the same again. He saw now that it is not just singing songs, but a sacred connection to God Himself. Amazing.

THE CORE

Chapter 19

WORSHIP CONNECTION

When you think of worship, many things may come to mind depending on your background. There are Sunday Church services, where we sing a few songs as part of the worship service. Worship may include many different postures, standing with hands raised high, kneeling or bowing down. Worship also includes the sacrifice of your life and daily surrender, and your obedience to God. Worship can look like many different things and contains many different elements.

For the purposes of this book, we will explore worship through music, songs of praise, and thanksgiving. We will discuss how to come before the throne of God to give him thanks, praise, honor, and glory.

Our goal is Core connection, connecting with God through worship. That is exactly what happened in this passage, "The trumpeters and musicians joined in unison to give praise and thanks to the LORD. Accompanied by trumpets, cymbals and other instruments, the singers raised their voices in praise to the LORD and sang: 'He is good; his love endures forever.' Then the temple of the LORD was filled with the cloud, and the priests could not perform their service because of the cloud, for the glory of the LORD filled the temple of God." (2 Chronicles 5:13-14) When worship went up, the glory of God came down and filled the temple. We can connect with God through worship.

This is a good time to say: NO, you are not exempt from worship just because you don't sing or play an instrument. So, for all the backrow, arms-crossed, non-singing churchgoers, you're going to have to step outside your comfort box to find the way God created you to worship Him. Here is an example in scripture of praise, without song, that Jesus accepted, "... the whole crowd of disciples began joyfully to praise God in loud voices for all the miracles they had seen: 'Blessed is the king who comes in the name of the Lord! Peace in heaven and glory in the highest!' Some of the Pharisees in the crowd said to Jesus, 'Teacher, rebuke your disciples!' 'I tell you,' he replied, 'if they keep quiet, the stones will cry out.'" (Luke 19:37-40) You see, we can use our voices to speak and shout the praises of God. Jesus doesn't want us to keep quiet!

GOD & WORSHIP

In the first section, Masters & Allegiance, we talked about choosing your master, your god. This becomes so important and obvious when it comes to worship. When you realize who or what your god is, you begin to see what you worship. Who or what gets your time, your money, your love, your desire, your focus is what you worship. If anything but God gets your worship, that's a problem. God said, "I am the LORD; that is my name! I will not yield my glory to another or my praise to idols." (Isaiah 42:8) God will not share His glory or praise with another.

God, our creator, understands our gravitation to a god and propensity to worship it. By His design we should be drawn to Him and worship Him. But, in case we miss the mark, He gave us the Ten Commandments. He begins by declaring who He is, "I am the Lord your God, who brought you out of Egypt, out of the land of slavery." (Exodus 20:2) Then, He gives the first two commandments with clear directions:

1. You shall have no other gods before me.
2. You shall not make for yourself an image in the form of anything in heaven above or on the earth beneath or in the waters below. You shall not bow down to them or worship them; for I, the Lord your God, am a jealous God, punishing the children for the sin of the parents to the third and fourth generation of those who hate me, but showing love to a thousand generations of those who love me and keep my commands. (Exodus 20:3-6)

God ties severe punishment or great blessings to who we choose to worship. We see this principle play out in the history of the Israelite people, beginning with Abraham.

God made a covenant with Abraham, "I will make you into a great nation…" (Genesis 12:2) That promise made Abraham the father of the nation of Israel and the Jewish people. God intended for Israel to be His own nation, a nation that would only worship Him, "You are to be holy to me because I, the Lord, am holy, and I have set you apart from the nations to be my own." (Leviticus 20:26) He desired to set them to be an example as a people and nation that God blesses and protects because they worship God and God alone.

But, Israel's loyalty waivered. They were not faithful to God and began to worship other gods. God said, "You shall have no foreign god among you; you shall not worship any god other than me. I am the LORD your God, who brought you up out of Egypt. Open wide your mouth and I will fill it. But my people would not listen to me; Israel would not submit to me. So, I gave them over to their stubborn hearts to follow their own devices." (Psalms 81:11-12)

We see this replay over and over again in scripture. When they turned from God to worship other gods, He would remove His hedge of protection and blessings from them. Their enemies would attack and overtake them. They would once again call on God to save them, repent, and seek God. God in His mercy would forgive them and draw them into His love and protection again. (Super short summary of 1&2 Kings and 1&2 Chronicles)

You see there are blessings and protection that come with drawing near God in worship. But God will not draw near those who worship other gods. In fact, it drew God's anger, "He served and worshiped Baal and aroused the anger of the Lord, the God of Israel, just as his father had done." (1 Kings 22:53) He allows us to choose who we worship. If we worship Him, we receive the blessings that come along it. But, if we choose to give our time, money, love, affection, and focus to other gods, God allows us to go.

The devil will gladly take your worship. He even tried to tempt Jesus, "Again, the devil took him to a very high mountain and showed him all the kingdoms of the world and their splendor. 'All this I will give you,' he said, 'if you bow down and worship me.'" (Matthew 4:8-9) Thankfully Jesus resisted the devil, and you can too. But first you need to realize...there is a battle for your worship.

WAR BEGINS & ENDS WITH WORSHIP

The spiritual battle between God and Satan began with worship and will end with worship. Satan began as Lucifer, an angel God created to worship Him before His throne. But, Lucifer took his worship from God, and placed it on himself, in the form of pride, "Your heart became proud on account of your beauty, and you corrupted your wisdom because of your splendor, So I threw you to the earth; I made a spectacle of you before kings." (Ezekiel 28:17)

Satan was thrown from heaven, along with the angels who chose to worship him instead of God, "Then war broke out in heaven. Michael and his angels fought against the dragon, and the dragon and his angels fought back. But he was not strong enough, and they lost their place in heaven. The great dragon was hurled down—that ancient serpent called the devil, or Satan, who leads the whole world astray. He was hurled to the earth, and his angels with him." (Revelation 12:7-9) And so, the war for worship began.

The final spiritual battle will end with worship. The Bible tells us that in the last days people will be forced to worship Satan, AKA the Beast, AKA the Anti-Christ (one world leader), "All inhabitants of the earth will worship the beast—all whose names have not been written in the Lamb's book of life, the Lamb who was slain from the creation of the world." (Revelation 13:8) That means that everyone on earth, whose name is not in Jesus's book of Life, will worship the beast, or Satan.

But, they won't just worship Satan, they will be REQUIRED to worship him, "The second beast was given power to give breath to the image of the first beast, so that the image could speak and cause all who refused to worship the image to be killed." (Revelation 13:15) Satan will force people to worship him or die. But, he also takes it a step further, "It also forced all people, great and small, rich and poor, free and slave, to receive a mark on their right hands or on their foreheads, so that they could not buy or sell unless they had the mark, which is the name of the beast or the number of its name." (Revelation 13:16-17) Not only will people be required to worship Satan; they will also be required to be branded with his name.

But, be warned, worshiping Satan is a fatal mistake, "A third angel followed them and said in a loud voice: 'If anyone worships the beast and its image and receives its mark on their forehead or on their hand, they, too, will drink the wine of God's fury, which has been poured full strength into the cup of his wrath. They will be tormented with burning sulfur in the presence of the holy angels and of the Lamb. And the smoke of their torment will rise for ever and ever. There will be no rest day or night for those who worship the beast and its image, or for anyone who receives the mark of its name.'" (Revelation 14:9-11) There are eternal consequences for worshiping Satan and taking his mark.

Though choosing not to worship Satan, at that time, will mean certain death, there are eternal rewards for those who remain faithful to, and worship God. The Bible says, "...And I saw the souls of those who had been beheaded because of their testimony about Jesus and because of the word of God. They had not worshiped the beast or its image and had not received its mark on their foreheads or their hands. They came to life and reigned with Christ a thousand years." (Revelation 20:4) Yes, there is a special reward for all those who endure, remain faithful, and worship God instead of Satan.

The spiritual battle for your worship is real and ongoing. The war continues in each of our lives. We each daily choose who we will worship. Most put little thought into the focus of their worship. But, who you worship, who you follow, who you obey has eternal consequences. It is worth thinking about, consciously choosing, and daily applying worship to God, and God alone.

WORSHIP IS KINGDOM CULTURE

The culture of heaven is so beautiful, alive, and filled with the presence of God. Everyone in heaven is there because they love the Lord. So, it only makes sense that worship is a large part of the culture of heaven.

You know that famous prayer that says, "... thy kingdom come, thy will be done on earth as it is in heaven"? Well, that was God, Jesus, teaching us to call down the kingdom of God into our earthly realm. The more we learn about heaven, God's kingdom, the culture, the practices, the habits of heaven, the more His kingdom will come, and His will be done on earth as it is in heaven.

So, if a large part of God's kingdom culture is worship, what does that look like? We see glimpses of heavenly worship in the book of Revelation, "the twenty-four elders fall down before him who sits on the throne and worship him who lives for ever and ever. They lay their crowns before the throne and say:

> *You are worthy, our Lord and God, to receive glory and honor and power, for you created all things, and by your will they were created and have their being. - Revelation 4:10-11*

What a beautiful picture of worship that honors God before His throne. But, how can we honor God with our worship here on earth?

WORSHIP THAT IS ACCEPTABLE TO GOD

The Bible is filled with scriptures we can use to guide our worship. There are many outward expressions of worship. We can worship God with singing, speaking, clapping, raising hands, dancing, painting, etc. But it must be more than that. Where does the outward expression of worship begin? What is your motivation? What is your goal? Jesus said, "Yet a time is coming and has now come when the true worshippers will worship the Father in Spirit and in truth, for they are the kind of worshipers the Father seeks. God is spirit, and his worshippers must worship in the Spirit and in truth." (John 4:23-24) God desires your heart and spirit to worship in truth.

We, as Prepared Warriors, desire to be "true worshipers" of God. Jesus spoke those words to a woman who was asking him about worship. When He mentions that "God is a spirit," He is reminding us that our own Spirits must connect with God's Spirit, the Holy Spirit, in worship. This worship connection occurs when you focus on God, when you pour out love to Him, when you give Him praise. You must worship with your spirit.

God looks at your heart when you worship. Jesus spoke with the teachers of the law, those who know the scriptures, and strictly follow the Jewish traditions. But Jesus saw them clearly, "These people honor me with their lips, but their hearts are far from me. They worship me in vain; their teachings are merely human rules." (Matthew 15:8-9) We can say all the right words, sing all the right notes, and still not please God. It is your heart God desires. It is your heart God will judge. You must worship God with your heart.

Imagine you are viewing a person worship God, but in the spirit, you can see colors flowing from their heart as they worship. Each vibrant flowing color is released from their heart as a gift to God. Then you see a thin white flow of color released from their mouth. That represents the sound coming from their voice, which is so small compared to the other large flowing bands of color. The greatest gifts we can give God in worship come from our hearts.

When we come to worship God, we acknowledge His greatness, His power, and His authority, "Therefore, since we are receiving a kingdom that cannot be shaken, let us be thankful, and so worship God acceptably with reverence and awe, for our 'God is a consuming fire.'" (Hebrews 12:28-29) God is not some small being who can be fooled with half-hearted compliments, flattery, or short-lived, short-focused praise.

When we approach the throne of God, to truly worship Him, we are advised to, "worship God acceptably with reverence and awe." That sets our minds to focus on God's sheer magnitude and authority over us. You must worship with your mind.

It is much easier to truly worship someone you are in awe of, than someone you're not that impressed with. If you're not that impressed with God, you've got some reading to do! Start at Genesis and keep going. There are things you will learn about God from His Word that will spur on your worship. Worship and the Word of God go hand in hand.

For Prepared Warriors, worship is a wonderful way to connect with God. When you come to worship God, focus on Him, and declare with your mouth the goodness of God, He is delighted. In 2 Chronicles 16:9 it says, "the eyes of the Lord look through the earth to find those whose hearts are Perfect toward him." God is looking for those who are looking for Him.

Worship is like waving a big flag to get His attention. He hears your praise going up, and His Spirit draws near. The more you pour into worship the more God's Spirit will pour into you. There is an open exchange that happens in the midst of worship. You open yourself up to reveal your heart and soul to God. He examines it, heals it, nourishes it, and restores it, all while you worship. There is little on earth that draws the manifest presence of God closer to us than worship. If you truly desire Core connection, worship is essential.

Chapter 20

WORSHIP
MEET - RELEASE - RECEIVE

Meeting with God in worship requires the uncluttering of our mind, and precise focus on God. The average church goer's mind wanders while worshiping God. They think about themselves, their problems, about their talent, or lack of talent. They think about their families, friends, the people around them, the worship team, critiquing their outfits, their hair, their voices. Their minds may wander to lunch, and what they will eat, or when they will sleep.

Worship may be considered as a start for the service, wishing it would be over, or go longer. All too often the focus during worship is on any and everything BUT God. It's a true miracle if any Core connection happens during worship time at church.

But worship is intended to be a time to come before God in adoration of who He is, and all He has done. Worship brings us before the throne of God, so that is where our minds should be, not perusing the room around us. But, to train your mind to focus squarely on God, forsaking all else, takes practice. Like an athlete the more you practice the better you will get. So, let the practice begin at the beginning.

How you begin worship is important. The Bible says, "Enter his gates with thanksgiving and his courts with praise; give thanks to him and praise his name." (Psalm 100:4) When you begin worship with thanking and praising God, your focus is forced to be on Him. You can only find the words to thank and praise God if you are thinking about who He is and all He has done.

You can start your worship time with speaking, shouting, or singing words of adoration to God. Again, the more you practice this, the easier it will become. If you have no idea what to say, fear not, you can speak or sing scriptures from the Bible. For example:

"Who among the gods is like you, LORD? Who is like you—majestic in holiness, awesome in glory, working wonders?" (Exodus 15:11)

"I will proclaim the name of the LORD. Oh, praise the greatness of our God! He is the Rock, his works are perfect, and all his ways are just. A faithful God who does no wrong, upright and just is he." (Deuteronomy 32:3-4)

"Blessed be your glorious name, and may it be exalted above all blessing and praise. You alone are the LORD. You made the heavens, even the highest heavens, and all their starry hosts, the earth and all that is on it, the seas and all that is in them. You give life to everything, and the multitudes of heaven worship you." (Nehemiah 9:3-6)

"For the LORD is good and his love endures forever; his faithfulness continues through all generations." (Psalm 100:5)

"In a loud voice they were saying: "Worthy is the Lamb, who was slain, to receive power and wealth and wisdom and strength and honor and glory and praise!" (Revelation 5:12)

"And they cried out in a loud voice: "Salvation belongs to our God, who sits on the throne, and to the Lamb." (Revelation 7:10)

"Amen! Praise and glory and wisdom and thanks and honor and power and strength be to our God for ever and ever. Amen!" (Revelation 7:12)

"We give thanks to you, Lord God Almighty, the One who is and who was, because you have taken your great power and have begun to reign." (Revelation 11:17)

Or, you can also declare who He is and thank Him for what He has done with your own words.

"You are the King of Kings, and the Lord of Lords. Nothing is more powerful than you!"

"God, you are the Good Shepherd. You never leave or forsake your children."

"God, you are faithful and true, full of goodness and mercy."

"God, you are worthy of all praise."

"Jesus, you are the Savior of the world, giving your life to save us."

"Holy Spirit you are wise counsel. You bless us over and over."

This mode of worship is the purest channel for worship, and focus on God. This worship is not dependent on the song you are singing, or if you know the song, or like the song, or anything about the song really. Declaring God's praise and honor should always precede the lyrics of any song. This is your personal worship to God. It is you directly telling your God, you, individually realize and are willing to say, that He is amazing.

You are choosing to focus on Him and give Him praise. Like the choice of salvation, no one can do this for you. To get the benefit of Core connection, you need to do this for yourself. Your choice to open your mouth and praise God will lead to your personal blessing.

Your personal praise can go on for the entire worship time. Continue to praise God and stay in this place of praise until you feel the Spirit of God move. Once the Spirit of God has arrived, or His attention is turned to your praise, that's a great time to sing to Him.

Next, you can worship God in song. But not all Christian songs are worship songs. Just as we are all created for different purposes, different songs have different purposes too. We use three categories to help define the type of song, and its best use: Throne Room Worship, Upward Worship, and Kingdom Songs.

1. THRONE ROOM WORSHIP

DEFINE: Songs to God, about God

Throne Room Worship songs are the highest form of worship. They provide the clearest, purest path to worship God, because He alone is the focus. The worship is not cluttered with our own problems, or feelings. These songs are an extension and continuation of the personal praise you begin with. They are completely focused on God, and exalting Him from a place of victory and authority, in His throne room.

CORE CONNECTION: Because this is the highest form of worship, it provides the best opportunity for Core connection. You can connect with God most easily by focusing completely on Him, while singing His praise.

WEAPON: Throne Room Worship is also a weapon against the enemy. This is true because simply worshiping God moves God to action on our behalf. It is also true when we draw close to God, He is our shield against the enemy. They cannot stand to come near us. It is also a weapon because we are actively focusing our minds on God, instead of the enemy, which lessens their power and authority over us.

EXAMPLES: Great is Thy Faithfulness (Thomas Chisholm), The Lion and the Lamb (Big Daddy Weave), King of Kings (Hillsong Worship)

There are wonderful examples of actual Throne Room Worship in the book of Revelation, beginning at chapter 4. The worship is completely focused on God. Throne Room Worship includes songs that praise God as the Father, as He is in heaven, they praise Jesus and His completed work on the cross, or they praise the Holy Spirit as the omniscience, omnipresent God. The purity of focus on God alone makes this category a smaller collection of songs. But, as the church begins to realize the power and importance of Throne Room Praise, we believe more songs will be written.

2. UPWARD WORSHIP

DEFINE: Songs to God, about God and how He helps us

Upward Worship is named such because we are directing our worship from earth to heaven. These songs relate the happenings of our earthly circumstances, and how God saves us. They are also considered worship. But these songs have a longer path to God, as we explore our circumstances, before or in the midst of worshipping God. These songs express our feelings and circumstances, then how God moved on our behalf.

CORE CONNECTION: Upward Worship songs can also be used for Core connection. The worship is directed to God, and about how He helps us, loves us, saves us. All of those things glorify and praise God.

WEAPON: Because these songs praise, worship and glorify God they are an effective weapon against the enemy. In fact, just placing yourself in a worship mindset, focusing on God, provides protection to you and disarms the enemy. Upward Worship songs help build your faith by remembering the truth of God's goodness, and that is a blow to the lies of the enemy.

EXAMPLES: Reckless Love (Cory Asbury), Amazing Grace (John Newton), So Will I (100 Billion X) (Hillsong UNITED)

There are examples of Upward Worship throughout Psalms, where David shares his great love for God. There are testimonials written after great events in the Bible: Exodus 15, Judges 5, 2 Samuel 22, etc. Love songs to God would also be Upward Worship, as they express our love for God, praising God for what He has done for us, how we love him, how He has helped us, saved us, delivered us.

3. KINGDOM SONGS

DEFINE: Not directed to God, but about Him, or His kingdom

Kingdom Songs are wonderful songs. They celebrate God, His kingdom or remind us who we are as children of God. These songs are not truly worship. It pleases God when we agree with Him and His kingdom principles, but these songs don't directly worship Him.

Who we sing about is who we focus on. The more we sing about ourselves, the less our focus is on God, the less it is worship. These songs still honor God, as we choose to agree with Him, they build our faith, and can be great declarations to recite.

CORE CONNECTION: Because these songs are not worship, they are not recommended for Core connection.

WEAPON: These songs can make great weapons against the enemy. Kingdom Songs can be a weapon against the enemy, because when we sing them, we come into agreement with God's kingdom (love, joy, peace, victory, forgiveness, faithfulness, etc.) and not the enemy's (fear, lies, anger, unforgiveness, doubt, etc.).

As we declare what God says, it breaks down the enemy's stronghold within us and around us. Then the healing can begin. There are some wonderful healing songs that are Kingdom Songs, and so important for Christians.

EXAMPLES: It is Well (Horatio Spafford), How He Loves (David Crowder Band), Break Every Chain (Tasha Cobbs)

Kingdom Songs include the great songs that carry special anointings. These songs may bring deliverance, healing, peace, strength, love, or joy. They may carry testimonies, or declarations that build our faith. Every song carries a spirit. If it isn't a worship song, but carries the spirit of God, it belongs to the Kingdom Songs category.

Our purpose with this book is Core connection, to truly meet with God. So, as you search for worship songs, look for Throne Room Worship or Upward Worship songs to get the best benefit out of your worship time with God.

After you have entered His gates with thanksgiving and praise, lifted up Throne Room worship to God, what comes next is up to God. This is the time where releasing and receiving happens. God deals with you as He sees fit. When you meet with God, it's always on His terms, His timeline, and His agenda. Our goal is to position ourselves in the best possible atmosphere, with our hearts, minds, and ears tuned to God.

Once God has moved as He intended, He will release you. Being able to discern and tune into God for what He is doing will come with practice and awareness. It is important not to go on and on and on with no regard for His agenda. This becomes self-indulgent, and makes the meeting about you, instead of God. Watch out for that trap.

Finally, if you commit to regular worship, it gives you a steady connection to God. It also alerts you when your connection is muddied or hindered, so you can take steps to repair your connection (see "Spiritual Keys" section). Meeting with God in worship enables a Core connection that will feed your soul, even as you praise Him.

RELEASE

Worship is a rare opportunity for us, the children of God, to give Him a gift. When you come to meet with God in worship, you are preparing your heart to open up to God, and let love, adoration, and praise flow to Him who is worthy. The first thing we release when meeting with God in worship is praise and worship. This is a pretty obvious one, but unfortunately isn't always accomplished. Use the previous guide to release your personal praise to God. Then, release praise to God with Throne Room or Upward Worship songs.

RELEASE THANKS

You can also release thanks to God in the midst of your worship. The Bible says, "Enter his gates with thanksgiving and his courts with praise; give thanks to him and praise his name." (Psalm 100:4) We focused on praise before, but giving thanks is equally important.

God is like a parent who enjoys their child's thankfulness and gratitude, but is unhappy with an ungrateful, spoiled, or complaining child. So, as you come to worship, "give thanks in all circumstances; for this is God's will for you in Christ Jesus." (1 Thessalonians 5:18) No matter where you may find yourself, thankfulness will bless God.

Job is the ultimate example in the Bible of one who suffered greatly here on earth. After losing all of his wealth, almost all of his servants, and all of his children dying, Job, "… fell to the ground in worship and said: 'Naked I came from my mother's womb, and naked I will depart. The LORD gave and the LORD has taken away; may the name of the LORD be praised.' In all this, Job did not sin by charging God with wrongdoing." (Job 1:20-22) Job could have easily cursed God and died, as his wife recommended. But instead he chose to praise the name of God, and in doing so, did not sin against God. Spoiler Alert: "The Lord blessed the latter part of Job's life more than the former part …" (Job 42:12)

Conversely, we have the story of the Israelite people. God performed miracle after miracle removing the Israelites from Egypt, and bringing them to the Promised Land. But they grumbled and complained the whole time, "Now the people complained about their hardships in the hearing of the LORD, and when he heard them his anger was aroused. Then fire from the LORD burned among them and consumed some of the outskirts of the camp." (Numbers 11:1) Grumbling and complaining brought God's anger. You don't want that! Thankfulness is so much better.

Paul shared his joy and thanks with the Philippians, "I rejoiced greatly in the Lord … I am not saying this because I am in need, for I have learned to be content whatever the circumstances. I know what it is to be in need, and I know what it is to have plenty. I have learned the secret of being content in any and every situation, whether well fed or hungry, whether living in plenty or in want." (Philippians 4:10-12) Whatever circumstances you find yourself in, choose to be thankful. Give thanks to God for any and everything you can bring to mind.

If you can't think of anything to thank God for in your own circumstances, thank God for who He is and what He has done, "I will give thanks to you, LORD, with all my heart; I will tell of all your wonderful deeds." (Psalm 9:1) Thank Him with your own words or with scripture, "Give thanks to the Lord, for he is good; his love endures forever." (1 Chronicles 20:34) Being able to thank God in the midst of trials sets you up for victory, hope, and faith. It blesses God when you release thanks to Him, declaring your blessings even when the battles rage against you.

RELEASE LOVE

One way we show our love for God is through worship. One of the most beautiful acts of worship in the Bible is found in Luke 7 when a sinful woman anoints Jesus with perfume. It says, "As she stood behind him at his feet weeping, she began to wet his feet with her tears. Then she wiped them with her hair, kissed them and poured perfume on them." (Luke 7:38)

Though this is a silent act of worship, it was warmly received by Jesus. He said, "Do you see this woman? I came into your house. You did not give me any water for my feet, but she wet my feet with her tears and wiped them with her hair. You did not give me a kiss, but this woman, from the time I entered, has not stopped kissing my feet. You did not put oil on my head, but she has poured perfume on my feet. Therefore, I tell you, her many sins have been forgiven – as her great love has shown. But whoever has been forgiven little loves little." (Luke 7:44-47)

Jesus was deeply moved by her passionate love for him. He received each act as her expression of love. He clearly tied her forgiveness to her love for him. Let your love be released to God through unapologetic worship.

RELEASE SIN & FORGIVENESS

As you connect with God through worship, His holy presence comes to meet with you. The holiness of God is a light on the dark areas of our hearts. Your sins become apparent. He highlights them, and calls you to turn from them. Some sins you may have forgotten about, or maybe didn't even realize it was a sin. But, once God shows it to you, you have the gift of repenting and releasing that sin.

It is the same with unforgiveness. God may highlight unforgiveness and call you to forgive those who have wronged you. He has given you the gift of forgiveness and released those who have wronged you. These are indeed gifts to you, see the section "Spiritual Keys" for more information. But regular repentance and forgiveness are also essential for Core connection.

Trying to worship God with sin and unforgiveness in your heart is like trying to sing with a big wad of gum in your mouth and earplugs in your ears. You can still do it, but it won't be as great as it could be. And at some point, it may completely stop you from singing at all! It's a hindrance; it gets in the way. If you just release, or spit out the gum, you can resume singing to the best of your ability. Once you spit out the gum, you'll realize your ears have been plugged! Sin hinders our ability to hear God. But, if you refuse to spit out the gum, it's a detriment to your worship and relationship with God. Spit out the gum, release your sin and unforgiveness, and connect with God more fully.

In 2 Chronicles 29 King Hezekiah orders the cleansing of the Temple of God, "The priests went into the sanctuary of the LORD to purify it. They brought out to the courtyard of the LORD's temple everything unclean that they found in the temple of the LORD. The Levites took it and carried it out to the Kidron Valley." (2 Chronicles 29:16)

Just as it was important for the Priests to cleanse God's Temple of everything unclean, it is important to keep yourself cleansed. Prepare yourself, "Don't you know that you yourselves are God's temple and that God's Spirit dwells in your midst?" (1 Corinthians 3:16) Release everything unclean, repent, and forgive. Then you can more easily connect to God through worship.

RECEIVE

In the midst of Core connection, connecting to God, the vine, the beautiful flow of connectivity begins. If you imagine your heart has a direct pipeline to God's heart. Once the connection is made beautiful, pure, hot, gold liquid flows from His heart to yours. This is the oil of God's anointing, "...He anointed us, set his seal of ownership on us, and put his Spirit in our hearts as a deposit, guaranteeing what is to come." (2 Corinthians 1:21-22)

This liquid is a healing balm to the wounds in your heart. It flows and covers hurt and pain. It seeks out and burns up sin and unforgiveness in your heart. It reaches into the depths of your heart's beliefs about God and about you, and releases truth straight from God's heart to yours. Then, once God has covered all He intends to cover, and all you allow Him access to, He leaves your heart covered in gold, His Spirit, until you connect with Him again.

This beautiful connection transpires whenever you truly open your heart to connect with God through His Word, Worship, and Prayer. It makes sense that God would release His heart to us through His Word. It even makes sense that He would release His heart when we pray. But, when we meet with God through worship, our intent is to come and release our praise to the God we love. We don't expect to receive from God when we worship. We have come to give to God. Worship is an offering, a gift you can give to God. But, God, who loves to give His children gifts, even ends up giving you His heart when you come to worship Him.

"If you, then, though you are evil, know how to give good gifts to your children, how much more will your Father in heaven give good gifts to those who ask him!" (Matthew 7:11)

RECEIVE LOVE

The first and greatest gift we receive from God when we worship is love. Waves of the goodness of God crash over you and make it difficult to stand. He reveals Himself, His goodness, His strength, His love to us as we worship. The more love you pour out to God in worship, the more love He responds with. It is the wonderful principle of reaping and sowing. God responds to love, because, "… God is love." (1 John 4:8)

If you feel unloved, rejected, or unworthy, worship should be your go-to in times of need. God has a way of correcting the lies and fears the enemy planted within you. His powerful weapon against the enemy is His great love for you. There is no denying it. Jesus said, "Greater love has no one than this; to lay down one's life for one's friends." (John 15:13) Jesus demonstrated the greatest act of love possible when He died on the cross for your sins. But, His love for you didn't stop there. God delivers a steady stream of love to those who connect to Him.

In the midst of worship, when God releases His spirit, the gold liquid to cover your heart, He is releasing His love to you. In the presence of pure love from the Father, the lies of the enemy begin to fall away, the fears the enemy planted begin to be uprooted. The truth is, "There is no fear in love. But perfect love drives out fear, because fear has to do with punishment. The one who fears is not made perfect in love. We love because he first loved us." (1 John 4:18-19) The more you know God, connect with God, receive love from God, the less fear you will have. And the beautiful thing about God's love is that it is never ending, "Give thanks to the Lord, for he is good; his love endures forever." (1 Chronicles 20:34) So, come, drink from the deep, unending well of God's love for you while you worship.

RECEIVE PEACE

Worship is a refuge for many people. When you meet with God, and sit at His feet in worship, you are leaving behind every burden, "Praise be to the Lord, to God our Savior, who daily bears our burdens." (Psalm 68:19) Just as the woman in Luke 7 sat at Jesus's feet, perfectly content to just be near Him, loving Him; we can have that peace and contentment as we draw near Christ in worship.

Meeting with God should always allow you to come rest in His presence, outside of any task list, or prayer list, or desperation we may feel in the moment. We are not children who place our own needs above acknowledging our King first. When we do leave all the worries of the day to ascend to the throne room to worship the King, the weight of our burdens is left behind. There, in the presence of God, He is most important. There we find the "peace of God, which transcends all understanding." (Philippians 4:7) You receive peace when you connect to God through worship.

RECEIVE HEALING

When you meet with God in worship, and Connect to the Core, you are opening yourself up to however God wants to heal you, in body, mind, or spirit. God made this promise to the Israelites, "Worship the LORD your God, and his blessing will be on your food and water. I will take away sickness from among you." (Exodus 23:25) God can bless those who worship Him with healing.

God can heal parts of you that are broken, parts that no one else can see. God can do in one worship setting, what would take you years in counseling to work through. God knows all the pieces of your story. He knows all the secrets of your heart. God shines a light on dark places, revealing and healing like no one else can. When your heart is open and connected to God, anything can happen.

Worship can even bring relief to those who are tormented by evil spirits, "Whenever the spirit from God came on Saul, David would take up his lyre and play. Then relief would come to Saul; he would feel better, and the evil spirit would leave him." (1 Samuel 16:23) When we worship God, our focus is on God, it's not on the enemy at all. But, a side benefit of true worship is that it is a weapon against the enemy, removing them, and bringing healing and relief to those who connect with God.

RECEIVE VICTORY

During worship our focus is on God, which places us in the atmosphere of victory, not fear or defeat. But while victory is rarely our goal or focus; it just happens to be an added benefit of worship! One of the greatest examples of victory in worship appears in a story found in 2 Chronicles 20. Three tribes joined together to attack Judah. Jehoshaphat, King of Judah, devised a plan, "After consulting the people, Jehoshaphat appointed men to sing to the LORD and to praise him for the splendor of his holiness as they went out at the head of the army, saying: 'Give thanks to the LORD, for his love endures forever.' As they began to sing and praise, the LORD set ambushes against the men of Ammon and Moab and Mount Seir who were invading Judah, and they were defeated. The Ammonites and Moabites rose up against the men from Mount Seir to destroy and annihilate them. After they finished slaughtering the men from Seir, they helped to destroy one another." (2 Chronicles 20:21-23)

Have you ever heard of such a thing? Their front line, as they went to battle, was singing and worshiping God. Have you ever seen that in a war movie? Have you ever read that strategy in your History books? What war could be won with just singers? Only God could do something this amazing. By placing God first, honoring and worshiping God, God won the battle for them. They didn't have to lift a finger against their enemy. It said, "the Lord set ambushes against the men." Isn't God amazing?

There is a great misconception that many Christians fall into. Many take on the world's wisdom in battle: Keep your eyes on the enemy. But, for Christians, the wisdom in battles is: Keep your eyes on God. If you keep your eyes on the enemy you may fall into fear, paranoia, and deception. But, if you keep your eyes on God, He gives you wisdom and insight into the enemy's plans. He keeps you in peace while the battle wages on. Just keeping your eyes on God will give you victory in battle. The easiest way to do that, is to worship your way through. Remember, "The LORD is my strength and my defense; he has become my salvation. He is my God, and I will praise him, my father's God, and I will exalt him." (Exodus 15:2) The Lord is your strength and defense. We don't wage war like the rest of the world. We wage war, and receive victory when we keep our eyes on God, worshipping our way through.

WORSHIP CONNECTION

Worship is inextricably tied to God. Worship is a tangible way of humbly posturing yourself before God in a state of love and gratitude. We should all desire to become true worshipers, who worship God in spirit, in truth, in reverence, and in awe. Those are the kind of worshipers the Father seeks.

The true Core connection occurs when we focus our hearts and minds on Christ and Christ alone. He deserves all the glory, all the honor, and all the praise. When we honor God in this way, He blesses us with His presence, and He always comes bearing gifts. We worship to give to God, but He ends up blessing us as well. This beautiful exchange allows God to fill you up, restore you, heal you, and love you. Learn to enjoy worship. It is a gift and a clear pathway to Core connection.

TAKE ACTION

Today is a great day to start worshiping God. There is no need to wait for the perfect time, or the perfect place, or the perfect circumstances, start now! There will always be a reason why you can't. Let's talk about how you can.

- Seek out worship warriors and worship with them (this is training)
- Worship first thing in the morning

- Worship on your way to work or school
- Worship while you shower, take advantage of the great acoustics
- Arrive on time to church, so you don't miss the worship time
- Train your heart and mind to focus on God alone

Just get started. You can refine the process later.

NOTE: The devil will try to come against you when you start to worship. Be prepared to withstand his attacks, of discouragement, busyness, etc. Plan now to NEVER GIVE UP!

> David sang to the LORD the words of this song
> when the LORD delivered him from the hand of all his
> enemies and from the hand of Saul. He said:
> The LORD is my rock, my fortress and my deliverer;
> my God is my rock, in whom I take refuge,
> my shield and the horn of my salvation.
> He is my stronghold, my refuge and my savior—
> from violent people you save me…
> He rescued me from my powerful enemy,
> from my foes, who were too strong for me.
> They confronted me in the day of my disaster,
> but the LORD was my support.
> He brought me out into a spacious place;
> he rescued me because he delighted in me.
> - 2 Samuel 22:1-3 and 18-20

THE CORE

146

PART 6
PRAYER CONNECTION

Chapter 21

TJ'S STORY
PRAYER POWER

The demons sat on the ledge outside TJ's house. Though they had been defeated on some fronts, they were sufficiently satisfied with the results of other attacks. At school they had shut TJ down. TJ wasn't sharing Jesus as much at school anymore. The kids were still taunting him and his permanent label of a "Jesus freak" had stuck. But he was still on their hit list, now that he was officially a part of the enemy camp.

TJ's angel, Nigel, remained by his side through everything. Nigel was proud of TJ's growth. Not every angel is assigned such willing participants in spiritual matters. Nigel was thankful that TJ wanted to know God better. When he found something that worked, he used it, like the scripture from his Pastor. TJ faithfully carried and memorized the scripture. It helped him on more than one occasion to remember God was with him.

Since TJ discovered God communicates with him during worship, he can't get enough of worshiping God. Those are Nigel's favorite moments, because he gets to worship too. And now Nigel has a new mission. TJ has not yet discovered the power of prayer. This one is always fun to introduce. Until now, TJ has tried to fight his school battles on his own. But eventually, Nigel knows, TJ will ask God for help.

TJ got up to get ready for school, just like any other morning. He hit the shower, struggling to wake up. He scrubbed his face while trying to remember if he completed all of his homework the night before. That triggered his memory of the mean kid in his science class, Drew, who just couldn't seem to leave TJ alone. Every day it was the same thing, "Look everyone, it's the Jesus freak. Got any new stories for us today? Maybe you can tell us again how he changed your life. Bring your Bible to school?" All this before the bell even rang. Of course, the other students laughed, after all he was the biggest kid in the class and no one wanted to become his next target.

TJ dreaded going to that class. Maybe I'll just stay home from school today, TJ thought. Knowing his mom would never go for it, he finished up his shower and headed to get dressed. As he sat down on the edge of his bed, just resting for a moment, he thought, maybe I should pray about it. What could it hurt? Nigel silently nodded in agreement. TJ said a quick prayer, "God I love you. I trust you to be my protector. Please protect me from Drew. Give me strength and courage. Amen." That was all TJ had in him, so it would have to do.

As TJ's mom pulled up to the school, she didn't notice his hesitation to get out. She was already preoccupied with her work, which kept calling with one emergency after another. He took a deep breath, and with a quick look up to the heavens, stepped out.

One by one TJ's classes ticked by. With his new approach of keeping his head down and not talking too much, most of his classmates barely even noticed him, and didn't give him any more trouble. But the minute he stepped into science class, Drew was waiting for him. Drew opened his mouth to start his verbal assault when the teacher interrupted, "Drew Anderson, you have been called to the office. Please take your books and all of your things with you." Drew gave one last glare at TJ but turned to get his bags and left the classroom! What just happened?

The demons were furious! They looked forward to their daily assault on TJ! What happened today? Where did TJ get that shield from? And where did their arrows go? None of them even hit TJ today!! They had Drew so well trained and prepared every day. They thought their work was done. They used a simple domino tactic on Drew. See, Drew's Dad and older brother spew abusive words at Drew to knock him down; then Drew uses abusive words to knock TJ down. The game could go on and on forever, if you set it up right. But it only takes one misplaced domino for the game to stop. AHHH! Back to the drawing board. We have to figure out what went wrong today!

Nigel looked up with a smile, "Thank you Father." It's amazing how one little prayer could open the door for more and more prayers.

TJ couldn't be happier. What a relief to sit through science class, which he actually liked, without the constant presence of Drew lurking close by. TJ felt his body relax, he took a deep breath, and closed his eyes for a second, "Thank you, God."

Throughout the day, TJ kept thinking about how one little prayer helped so much. What would happen if TJ started praying every morning? TJ hadn't really thought about prayer as being too important before, but maybe it was.

That night as he went to bed, his mind drifted to God, "God I don't really know you. I want to get to know you. I want to learn all there is about you. I want to understand you, and how you work. You are so much greater than I am. I'm still learning. But I want to know. I want to know you, and act in ways that please you, because I love you." With that, he went to sleep.

TJ found something so powerful! He didn't know the power yet, but he would soon learn that praying to God was more potent than any enemy he would face. If one simple prayer blocked his enemy, imagine what daily prayer could do in his life! This was just the beginning!

THE CORE

Chapter 22

PRAYER CONNECTION

Prayer is the most widely discussed and accepted spiritual practice. It is a part of most religions. There are books, sermons, teaching and songs about prayer. We often hear, "I'm praying for you," or, "You are in our thoughts and prayers." It is so common, that to many people it has become benign. But still many others realize, at least on the surface, that prayer is important, and powerful.

The gift of prayer is really quite extraordinary. Prayer supposes that we, mere mortals, are given the right, and the privilege to actually talk to God. God is the Creator, supreme power, and authority that presides over all things, from such a high state that we are unable to see Him in our realm. How can our simple thoughts, and spoken words travel the distance and space between us and God, to hit His ears and cause Him to respond? It is a truly amazing and utterly baffling connection for communication. Prayer is beyond our understanding.

It takes great faith to believe that this communication is indeed taking place. Yet, most people engage in the act of prayer without a second thought, and never doubting God will hear them. It is as if God has planted the knowledge and faith for prayer within our very beings. That we could talk to Him, and that He will listen.

But, from there, things get a little more complicated. Everyone has a different experience with prayer. Some go about their day never considering prayer, until a tragedy disrupts them. Then the need for prayer exists, but how to do it, and where to start is a mystery. They may try to stumble their way through, or just ask others to pray for them.

Our relationships with prayer are as vast as our relationships with God. Some believe prayer is reserved for the most spiritual, or righteous among us, of which they are not. So, prayer never touches their lips. For some people, and religious groups, prayers are memorized, or recited, as a formula to speak to receive what they need, or to bring forgiveness of sin. Some pray only in dire circumstances, as a last cry for help. There are others who love God but aren't sure how to pray. They are unsure how to start. There may be confusion over what prayer is, and why or how we should pray. God's will is going to be done anyway, right?

For Prepared Warriors, prayer is a path to Core connection. Truly connecting with God through prayer is where the power, the blessing, the peace, the joy, and the life resides. There is a time for a simple urgent prayer. There is a time for prayers of petition. But, as a regular practice, prayer connection is how you will find God, who holds the key to all you need. "But seek first his kingdom and his righteousness, and all these things will be given to you as well." (Matthew 6:33)

Until you experience God's presence in prayer, you have not experienced Core connection through prayer. Fear not! This is the first step toward learning to truly connect with God through prayer.

Chapter 23

JESUS & PRAYER

As always, Jesus sets a wonderful example for us. Jesus spent time in prayer and Jesus taught about prayer. Jesus gave us examples in how, when and where he prayed. If Jesus prayed, though He is God, and is divinely connected and one with God the Father and the Holy Spirit, how much more important is it for us to pray? Jesus surely has heavenly insight into how to pray, and specifically how to connect to God through prayer. So, as always, we start with Jesus.

Jesus regularly departed from his disciples and followers to go and pray. Word about Jesus spread, and the crowds around him grew, "But Jesus often withdrew to lonely places and prayed." (Luke 5:16) Jesus led by example, "After he had dismissed them, he went up on a mountainside by himself to pray. Later that night, he was there alone." (Matthew 14:23) We often see Jesus finding a quiet place to pray. When he went by himself to pray, He was preparing himself to meet with and hear from God the Father.

Jesus prayed at various times in the day. Sometimes He prayed in the morning, "Very early in the morning, while it was still dark, Jesus got up, left the house and went off to a solitary place, where he prayed. (Mark 1:35) Jesus prayed in the evening in Gethsemane, even as his disciples fell asleep.

Sometimes Jesus would pray through the night, "One of those days Jesus went out to a mountainside to pray, and spent the night praying to God. When morning came, he called his disciples to him and chose twelve of them, whom he also designated apostles." (Luke 6:12-13) There is not one specific time to pray. Whenever you feel called to pray, whenever you want to meet with God, find a quiet place and pray! Whatever time of day works for you to have regular prayer time with God, set it apart, keep it holy, and pray.

There are different reasons to pray, and topics to pray about. Jesus prayed for others, "My prayer is not that you take them out of the world but that you protect them from the evil one." (John 17:15) He prayed for His disciples, for all believers, and he prayed for children, "Then people brought little children to Jesus for him to place his hands on them and pray for them..." (Matthew 19:13)

Jesus also prayed for himself. We see a piece of his poignant prayer just before He would be betrayed, tortured, and crucified, "Going a little farther, he fell with his face to the ground and prayed, 'My Father, if it is possible, may this cup be taken from me. Yet not as I will, but as you will.'" (Matthew 26:36-39) Then Jesus, "... went away a second time and prayed, 'My Father, if it is not possible for this cup to be taken away unless I drink it, may your will be done.'" (Matthew 26:42) Jesus came to His Father in prayer in his time of need. He asked for God to take the "cup" or trial from Him. But, conceded that God the Father's will should be done.

Imagine having to endure this heavy burden of knowing your impending death, and each blow that would proceed it. Imagine the weight of the world Jesus felt on his shoulders. His closest friends could not shoulder that burden for him or with him. They couldn't even stay awake as Jesus prayed.

God...He could talk to God. He could meet with God. He could pray to God, the only one who could take the cup from Him. He could talk to God, who is certain to give him wise counsel, comfort, and peace even in the midst of the trial. Jesus knew where to go and who to talk to in his time of need, because He had been there so many times before. He went to meet with His Father.

This is such an important example for us to see Jesus praying in his time of great distress. We will all surely face life's battles, some that will make us fall with our faces to the ground in prayer like Jesus. Isn't it reassuring to know Jesus has walked that same path? He has endured unimaginable distress and He turned to God in prayer. So, we can be assured that we too can do the same thing.

When we think of Jesus praying, the most famous prayer is, "The Lord's Prayer," found in Matthew 6 and Luke 11. But there is a wonderful prayer from Jesus in John 17. This is Jesus's longest, most complete prayer found in scripture. This passage is worthy of a study of its own. This prayer or conversation with God is like a daily report. He is coming to God to discuss the work He completed for the Father. He shows that he cared for his disciples and asks God to protect them after He leaves. Then he closes with a prayer for all believers. Jesus desires that they would be united, and completely connected to God the Father. Jesus connects with God through prayer and so should we. The best way to have a relationship with someone is to talk to them on a regular basis. So, prayer is an essential part of having a real relationship with God. Jesus knew that and showed us that truth.

JESUS TAUGHT

Jesus didn't just pray, he also taught others to pray. On one occasion his disciples, those closest to him, saw his regular prayer life, and asked him to teach them how to pray. This is where Jesus gave some wonderful and important guidelines to prayer, and also gave them the example of "The

Lord's Prayer." Jesus taught them to pray like this, "Our Father in heaven, hallowed be your name, your kingdom come, your will be done, on earth as it is in heaven. Give us today our daily bread. And forgive us our debts, as we also have forgiven our debtors. And lead us not into temptation, but deliver us from the evil one." (Matthew 6:9-13) There is a lot packed into that little prayer so let's unpack it.

For those new to prayer, isn't it wonderful that Jesus didn't give us a long, complex, or difficult example of how to pray? He gave us a prayer that is so simple, a child can understand it and recite it, yet so thorough, the prayer can be used by any person in the world, in any circumstance, and it will fit their needs. In fact, Jesus taught against babbling on and on, "And when you pray, do not keep on babbling like pagans, for they think they will be heard because of their many words. Do not be like them..." (Matthew 6:7) The number of our words does not affect the outcome of our prayers. That is sure to be a relief to those who are less talkative! Jesus continued, "...for your Father knows what you need before you ask him." (Matthew 6:7-8) God knows your every need, just go ahead and ask Him for it.

Jesus warned us that prayer isn't something to be used to garner admiration or some kind of spiritual superiority. He said, "And when you pray, do not be like the hypocrites, for they love to pray standing in the synagogues and on the street corners to be seen by others. Truly I tell you, they have received their reward in full. But when you pray, go into your room, close the door and pray to your Father, who is unseen. Then your Father, who sees what is done in secret, will reward you." (Matthew 6:5-6) He himself followed this sound advice. His prayer time with God took place in solitude. He didn't parade his prayers around like they were some kind of show for other people to marvel at. Jesus advises us to find a quiet place to go and meet with God. It is not the longest, loudest, most beautiful prayers that are required. It is the desire to connect with God, and an honest cry for help, that brings Him to you.

God clearly intended his house, his temple, his church to be a place where we can come and meet with God in prayer. When this holy place is used for sinful purposes, God is moved to anger, "Jesus entered the temple courts and drove out all who were buying and selling there. He overturned the tables of the money changers and the benches of those selling doves. 'It is written,' he said to them, "My house will be called a house of prayer," but you are making it a den of robbers.'" (Matthew 21:12-13) The importance and holiness of prayer is dear to God's heart. He could have made his house a house of celebration, a house of meeting, a house of worship, a house of preaching. But instead, He declared it to be a house of prayer.

THE KINGDOM OF GOD AND PRAYER

Jesus certainly knew how to pray, and how we should pray. He is God, and importantly He understands how His kingdom works. In the book of Revelation, we see a beautiful picture of how our prayers are handled in heaven, "Another angel, who had a golden censer, came and stood at the altar. He was given much incense to offer, with the prayers of all God's people, on the golden altar in front of the throne. The smoke of the incense, together with the prayers of God's people, went up before God from the angel's hand." (Revelation 8:3-4) Isn't that amazing? Our prayers are collected in heaven and placed before the throne of God.

Your prayers are like a gift offered to God and they are precious to Him. But God doesn't just sit on His throne far above us and far from us. No, prayer actually causes God to come and draw closer to us. The Israelites realized this, "What other nation is so great as to have their gods near them the way the LORD our God is near us whenever we pray to him?" (Deuteronomy 4:7) That's an amazing aspect of prayer. God draws near to us when we pray.

God said, "Then you will call on me and come and pray to me, and I will listen to you. You will seek me and find me when you seek me with all your heart. I will be found by you," declares the LORD." (Jeremiah 29:12-13) God is waiting to meet with you. He listens, and He draws near to you when you pray.

As we learn how to approach the throne of God through prayer, it is important to note that God's kingdom has laws and order. Thankfully, God gives us grace and room to learn and grow. He does not expect a new Christian to be able to understand all of His ways right away. However, as part of the maturing process for each Christian, we should seek to better understand God and how His kingdom works.

There is a proper way to approach the King, a protocol for preparing yourself to speak to the King, and a proper time and way to present your requests to the King. As you learn and grow in your understanding of God and His kingdom, your prayer life will improve, and your prayer connection to God will ignite.

As you go to pray, the steps and order of your prayer have meaning. Prepared Warriors encourage the use of the acronym PRAY (Praise, Repent, Ask, Yield). So, as with worship, we begin prayer with praise, followed by a time of repentance and forgiveness. Then, you ASK and present your requests to God.

Finally, it is important to yield, stop, and hear from God. He is always speaking; we must learn to stop and listen. Though this prayer structure is a great guide it is not an exact science or a required formula for each prayer. The Holy Spirit is always the leader. As you learn to listen, you begin to yield more and more frequently in prayer. This is a good place to start.

158

Chapter 24

P - R - A - Y
(Praise - Repent - Ask - Yield)

P - PRAISE

The proper way to approach the King is with thanksgiving and praise, "Enter his gates with thanksgiving and his courts with praise; give thanks to him and praise his name. For the Lord is good and his love endures forever; his faithfulness continues through all generations." (Psalms 100:4-5) When you come to meet with God, to seek Him, to have your prayers heard in the throne room of the most high, any old greeting just won't do! When you start your prayer with praise, you are acknowledging the great and high position of the Lord. You are showing Him honor, respect, and love. Praising God also shows humility and a spirit that is ready to follow God's will above your own.

When you praise God, you draw his attention and alert him to your desire to communicate with him in a most inviting way. If you wanted to have a conversation with someone important, you wouldn't yell across the room at them or start talking to them without a proper greeting. If you had something important to talk to them about, you would want to be sure they are tuned in and ready to talk. If you had to, you would seek them out, go to them, say their name, then sit and talk with them face to face. It is the same with prayer. God is THE MOST important being you will ever communicate with. Don't let that scare you into silence. Let it be a guide to how you begin your prayers.

The praise we give God is not shallow or meaningless. But the more you come to know God, the easier it is to praise Him with great depth and meaning, as you remember His goodness and faithfulness in your own life. It works to say your own words, words from a song, or reciting a scripture to praise God. It is fun to look for and collect praiseworthy phrases and scriptures to use in your prayer time.

Our Father in heaven, hallowed be your name, your
kingdom come, your will be done, on earth as it is in heaven.
Give us today our daily bread. And forgive us our debts, as
we also have forgiven our debtors. And lead us not into
temptation, but deliver us from the evil one.
- Matthew 6:9-13 underline added

The Lord's Prayer begins with praise. Jesus begins with acknowledging God's greatness in heaven. Then, He follows that up by saying God's name is holy. The prayer continues to declare that God's kingdom will come, and His will be done on earth as in heaven. That passage speaks of God's authority and power over heaven and earth. Praise starts the prayer by setting up a clear picture of who God is, and what honor He deserves. That's the way to start your prayer.

PRAY OUT LOUD

PRAISE: I praise you God most high. You are king of kings and lord of lords. You are above all things. Nothing stands up to you, but all things fall to you. You are patient, and full of grace and mercy. You are full of goodness, kindness and love. Your love for me endures forever. (add your own words)

* See examples of praise in the Worship Connection Chapter.

Thanksgiving is also included in this part of your prayer. Thanking God with a grateful heart for all He has done endears us to God. Much like an earthly father, God the Father, loves to see that His children are thankful and grateful. He does not like grumbling and complaining. So, when you are beginning your prayers with praise, include your thankfulness.

Thank God for the big things and the little things. As you begin to notice and thank God for the small blessings in your life, you'll see those blessings begin to multiply! It is true that, "Every good and perfect gift is from above, coming down from the Father of the heavenly lights, who does not change like shifting shadows." (James 1:17) So, keep thanking God. He loves to bless you.

PRAY OUT LOUD

THANKSGIVING: Thank you, God, for dying on the cross for my sins. Thank you for loving me even before I knew you. Thank you for your beautiful creation. Thank you for my friends and my family. Thank you for _____, _____, _____. (add your own words)

R - REPENT & FORGIVE

The protocol for cleansing and preparing yourself to speak to the King is repenting of your sins and forgiving those who hurt you. It is not wise to step into the throne room of the Most High God with an unclean spirit. And you are unclean, "for all have sinned and fall short of the glory of God." (Romans 3:23) Pretending to be something you are not doesn't work with God. He sees all and knows all. You can't fool him, and you can't skip this step if you want him to hear and answer your prayers. But repentance and forgiveness are gifts. They truly are.

God allows us the luxury of a spiritual bath. It is an honor to have God remove all the dirt and debris our souls have accumulated. For a new Christian, this process can be long and arduous. But it is the redeeming work of the cross. Meaning, Jesus died so your sins would be forgiven. With each sin you confess before God, as He forgives you, your love for Him grows deeper. As you see God's willingness to forgive even the most heinous sins, you can't help but be left in awe and wonder at He who loves you so much!

God expects us to willingly forgive those who have sinned against us, as He forgives us. It may seem unreasonable sometimes to forgive someone who has truly hurt you. But it benefits you greatly to forgive and release hurt, anger, and bitterness. Holding onto those things weighs down your soul, spirit, and even your body. As you forgive them and release them to God, a great weight is lifted off of you. Then you truly realize that God's forgiveness is a gift to you.

As wonderful and important as this spiritual bath is, it serves a specific purpose for prayer. Unconfessed sin hinders your prayers, "But your iniquities have separated you from your God; your sins have hidden his face from you, so that he will not hear." (Isaiah 59:2) God won't hear your prayers when you hold onto your sin. He will hide his face from you. By holding onto your sin, you show God the sin is more important to you than God. He will not be second place in your life. Confess your sin, leave it at the foot of the cross, then run to Jesus.

PRAY OUT LOUD

REPENTANCE: Search my heart, O God, and show me every sinful thought, word, or action I have committed against you. I confess _____, _____, _____, _____. God please remove all unholy things and people from my life. Father please forgive me and help me to turn from sin to You.

Forgiveness is equally important for prayer. Jesus said, "And when you stand praying, if you hold anything against anyone, forgive them, so that your Father in heaven may forgive you your sins." (Mark 11:25) God tells you to stop your prayers to forgive someone. Forgiveness is that important to God.

Forgiveness is crucial. Jesus said, "For if you forgive other people when they sin against you, your heavenly Father will also forgive you. But if you do not forgive others their sins, your Father will not forgive your sins." (Matthew 6:14-15) Don't you want God to forgive your sins? Then, stop your prayers, and forgive anyone you need to forgive.

Our Father in heaven, hallowed be your name, your kingdom come, your will be done, on earth as it is in heaven. Give us today our daily bread. <u>And forgive us our debts, as we also have forgiven our debtors</u>. And lead us not into temptation, but deliver us from the evil one.
- Matthew 6:9-13 underline added

The Lord's prayer includes repentance and forgiveness. We ask God to, "forgive us our debts." That is a way of asking God to forgive our sins. Then, the next phrase, "as we also have forgiven our debtors," says that we are forgiving those who sin against us. Jesus included these important phrases because they are important kingdom principles and should be a part of our regular prayer life.

PRAY OUT LOUD

FORGIVENESS: Heavenly Father please bring to my mind anyone I need to forgive. Help me to forgive them from the depths of my soul. I forgive _____ for _____. (repeat until you have forgiven everyone for everything, large and small) As I forgive others, I ask that you forgive me of my sins.

* Repentance and Forgiveness are big topics that are covered in greater detail in Book 2: "Weapons & Armors, Prepared Warriors."

A - ASK

Now is the proper time to present your requests to the King. Though it is tempting to start your prayers at this step, it is not wise to start here. Rather, after you greet God with thanksgiving and praise, and you have been spiritually cleansed, this is the time to present your request. Now, His ears are open and ready to hear how He can bless you, His child. Oh, the many requests and petitions we can place before the throne of God. Oh, the burdens we needlessly carry.

Come, bring that request to God, and leave it there. We are not created to carry these burdens. God always intended for us to come to Him with our every need. He is our provider, our healer, our counselor, our defender, our shelter, our everything.

God truly delights in giving you the best. Jesus said, "Which of you fathers, if your son asks for a fish, will give him a snake instead? Or if he asks for an egg, will give him a scorpion? If you then, though you are evil, know how to give good gifts to your children, how much more will your Father in heaven give the Holy Spirit to those who ask him!" (Luke 11:11-13) You see God really loves you. He is a good Father who knows how to give good gifts to His children.

As you draw closer to God, it brings Him glory to answer your prayers. You can ask for anything, "If you remain in me and my words remain in you, ask whatever you wish, and it will be done for you. This is to my Father's glory, that you bear much fruit, showing yourselves to be my disciples." (John 15:7-8) God wants you to bear much fruit. Imagine if Jesus's disciples went around asking God to heal people and no one was healed. That wouldn't bring God glory. But it delights God to be glorified through you and your requests.

God, who knows our hearts, weighs our motives while we pray, "When you ask, you do not receive, because you ask with wrong motives, that you may spend what you get on your pleasures." (James 4:2-3) Asking God for material possessions for greed or pride is not a good idea. So, check your heart; check your motives.

For many people this is the easiest step. We are used to asking God for what we need. But there are a few things to consider when you come before God with your requests:

1. ASK ACCORDING TO HIS WILL

Here on earth here there are three forces at work, our own free will, Satan's will, and God's will. God has given us free will to make our own choices in how we will live. His desire is that we will choose Him and live according to His will. But our free will sometimes aligns with Satan's will and results in evil throughout the earth. The best-case scenario is when we lay down our will, ignore Satan's will, and follow God's will.

Sometimes it's hard to know God's will. But, in that case your prayer becomes even simpler, "God let your will be done." That's it. Just ask that His plan, His will to be done for the person or circumstance you are praying for. You can trust and be sure that God's will is right. God is always right. The Lord's prayer gives us this example:

> *Our Father in heaven, hallowed be your name, your kingdom come, <u>your will be done</u>, on earth as it is in heaven. <u>Give us today our daily bread</u>. And forgive us our debts, as we also have forgiven our debtors. <u>And lead us not into temptation, but deliver us from the evil one</u>. - Matthew 6:9-13 underline added*

In this prayer, Jesus teaches us to ask for God's will to be done. He also asks for God to provide "our daily bread" for our physical and spiritual needs. Jesus asks God to protect us from temptation and the evil one. These are general requests that give us a solid foundation to ask God for those things. We can ask God to provide. We can ask God to protect us. And we can ask for His will to be done.

When we pray according to God's will we can be confident that God hears and answers our prayers. Be bold, "This is the confidence we have in approaching God: that if we ask anything according to his will, he hears us. And if we know that he hears us – whatever we ask – we know that we have what we asked of him." (1 John 5:14-15) The more you know God, the more confident you will be in your prayers.

Through reading His word you begin to understand how God works. You read and learn His decisions in the past. It helps you understand how He may respond in your situation. Then, you can be confident when you pray, that you know the Father, and you can agree with His will in prayer.

Sometimes it appears God's will bring judgment. God, after all, is a just God who does not endure evil to go unpunished. The natural consequences of sin on the earth should not be mistaken as God's will. It is true that sometimes God's will brings judgment, but God prefers mercy. Every prophet in the Bible, brings a warning to the people choosing evil. They tell of coming judgment from God. But, every time God offers them mercy if they will repent, "… Mercy triumphs over judgment." (James 2:13)

So, even if judgment is deserved, we can still ask for God's mercy. Some examples in scripture are Abraham petitioning God to spare the evil cities of Sodom and Gomorrah. The angels came to fulfil God's will, but Abraham still asked God for mercy if only ten righteous people could be found in the city. But ten were not found. (Genesis 18:16-33)

Another example is Moses pleading with God not to destroy the Israelite people who had just sinned by making and worshiping idols. Moses interceded and God relented. (Exodus 32:9-14)

The point is, we can make a request, but it is up to God how he will answer. His decision, His will is still the final answer. And we can trust that He knows best, even when we don't understand.

"For my thoughts are not your thoughts, neither are my ways your way," declares the Lord. "As the heavens are higher than the earth, so are my ways higher than your ways and my thoughts your thoughts." - Isaiah 55:8-9

2. ASK IN FAITH

Can God do what you ask? Your requests are as big as your faith. Meaning, if you only believe God will move in small ways in your life, or in your world, then you only ask for small things. Or maybe you believe God helps other people, but not you. Then, your faith in God isn't complete and you won't ask God for what you really want or need.

You may rely on your own strength to provide your need, instead of having faith God will provide for you. But James reminds us, "You do not have because you do not ask God." (James 4:2) Is your faith in God or yourself?

You can tell a lot about your faith in God, by what you ask from Him. The Bible tells us, God "… is able to do immeasurably more than all we ask or imagine, according to his power that is at work within us." (Ephesians 3:20) So, even when you pray your biggest prayer, asking for the grandest thing, God can top that! Really! God is all powerful, He can do immeasurably more than all we can ask or even imagine! So, ask big! Have big faith!

Did you know doubting God actually hinders your prayers? We are told, "But when you ask, you must believe and not doubt, because the one who doubts is like a wave of the sea, blown and tossed by the wind. That person should not expect to receive anything from the Lord." (James 1:6-7) Pray with faith that God will answer your prayers.

Jesus gives us a great illustration of how our faith in God affects our prayers. Truly I tell you, if anyone says to this mountain, 'Go, throw yourself into the sea,' and does not doubt in their heart but believes that what they say will happen, it will be done for them. Therefore, I tell you, whatever you ask for in prayer, believe that you have received it, and it will be yours." (Mark 11:22-24) As you pray, and the words come out of your mouth, check your faith, and decide to firmly agree that God can and will answer your prayer.

"Truly I tell you, if you have faith and do not doubt, not only can you do what was done to the fig tree, but also you can say to this mountain, 'Go, throw yourself into the sea,' and it will be done. If you believe, you will receive whatever you ask for in prayer." (Matthew 21:21-22)

3. BE PERSISTENT

Sometimes we believe God to be like our earthly authority. We don't want to bother him with our meager requests, or trouble him with our persistence. But Jesus told us otherwise. He said, "...Suppose you have a friend, and you go to him at midnight and say, 'Friend, lend me three loaves of bread; a friend of mine on a journey has come to me, and I have no food to offer him.' And suppose the one inside answers, 'Don't bother me. The door is already locked, and my children and I are in bed. I can't get up and give you anything.' I tell you, even though he will not get up and give you the bread because of friendship, yet because of your shameless audacity he will surely get up and give you as much as you need." (Luke 11:5-8) That's right! Jesus taught us to use "shameless audacity" when asking for what we need. That is actually how we should pray.

Jesus also gave the illustration of the persistent widow, who continued to daily bring her requests to a judge. Though he was an unjust judge, even he would give in to the widow's persistence. He concludes by saying, "And will not God bring about justice for his chosen ones, who cry out to him day and night? Will he keep putting them off? I tell you; he will see that they get justice, and quickly..." (Luke 18:7-8) God, who is just, hears us pleading with him over and over, and is moved to act on our behalf.

Jesus not only gives us permission to keep asking God, He himself demonstrates persistence in his own prayers. The night before his crucifixion, Jesus asked God two times, "My Father, if it is possible, may this cup be taken from me. Yet not as I will, but as you will." (Matthew 26:39) Even in Jesus's persistence, He concedes to the will of the Father. Don't hold back, trying to be meek with your request. Keep asking God! So, what can you ask God for in prayer?

- Ask God for your personal needs.
- Ask God to help your friends and family.
- Ask God to help your community, state or country.
- Ask God for salvations and spiritual growth
- Ask God for protection
- Ask God for healing
- Ask God for provisions

- Ask God for counsel
- Ask God for justice
- Ask God for His Kingdom to come, and His will to be done.

PRAY OUT LOUD

ASK: God, my Father, I am asking that Your will be done in my life. I trust you; I believe you, and I have faith that you will move in my life. Your word says, "And we know that in all things God works for the good of those who love him, who have been called according to his purpose." (Romans 8:28) God I love you, and I have been called according to your purpose. I believe you will work all things for the good in my life.

So, I say to you: Ask and it will be given to you; seek and you will find; knock and the door will be opened to you. For everyone who asks receives; the one who seeks finds; and to the one who knocks, the door will be opened. - Luke 11:9-10

Y - YIELD

Our final step in prayer is to yield, stop, or listen. God, our heavenly Father, has come to meet with you, has received your praise, listened to your confession, taken your requests, and now it is only fitting that you stop and let Him speak. He is, after all, the King. He granted you access to Him, so don't leave before you get blessed, get counseled, get your answer. What God says is infinitely more important than anything we say. So, why do we usually do all the talking?

For Prayer Connection, your goal is to meet with God through prayer. We use the act of prayer to strengthen our relationship with God. Prayer Connection is not an opportunity to dump all your worries on him in a stream of conscious monologue, barely stopping for a breath, let alone stopping to listen. If you don't stop to allow God to be involved in the conversation, what kind of relationship is that? You have missed the goal.

In any good relationship, communication is key. Engaging in regular conversation, where both parties speak and are heard is essential. With the give and take of conversation you learn more about the other person.

As we mentioned in the beginning of this chapter, God may lead you to yield at other times throughout your prayer. So, it's important to tune into

His Spirit, and yield as He leads. Let's consider a few different settings that are comparable to communication with God:

- When speaking to a friend, the communication flows back and forth between friends. There is genuine love and affection in the conversation. Friends share their hearts and desires with one another and depart with well wishes.

- In a family setting, where a child comes to seek wise counsel from his/her father, the child shares the burdens and troubles of their heart. Then, the child will wait eagerly to hear the wisdom from their father.

- In a classroom setting, the student comes to class to hear from the wise teacher. The student is allowed to ask questions but listens most of the time. The students remain in the classroom until the teacher excuses them.

- Then, we consider approaching the King. Once you are allowed an audience with the King, you enter giving him honor. Then, you may speak your requests, but you would never leave before the King has responded! You always wait for a response and would stay until you are excused.

In each scenario, there is a clear exchange that occurs. Like with friends, it is an equal level of exchange. In the example with the father, you may speak more, but wait to hear his counsel. In the classroom, God, the teacher is given the floor to teach and instruct you. And finally, with God as King, you have come to receive an audience with the highest authority, wait patiently for His response. In each example, listening is important.

The art of listening takes practice and discipline. But the idea of yielding to hear from God, who is invisible to us, may seem weird at first. This prayer step will take some intentional practice. Yes, you need to practice waiting. That's what it takes to meet with God, "Be still before the LORD and wait patiently for him..." (Psalm 37:7) When you come before the throne, you give up your agenda, your schedule, your control, and surrender to His timing, His agenda, His schedule, and His control. It takes practice, repetition, and discipline to consciously stop and wait on God.

It will cost your time. Any true, good relationship requires time, focus, and attention. But, investing time into a relationship with God is the best investment you can make, because it yields everlasting blessings in this life and the next. As you sow time in His presence, God will extend your time.

As you slow down and wait on the Lord. You are waiting to hear from God. You may be asking, "Does God really speak to us?" Scripture clearly shows that God speaks to us. As usual, we start with Jesus, "When all the people were being baptized, Jesus was baptized too. <u>And as he was praying,</u>

heaven was opened, and the Holy Spirit descended on him in bodily form like a dove. And a voice came from heaven: 'You are my Son, whom I love; with you I am well pleased.'" (Luke 3:21-22 underline added) God spoke to Jesus as He prayed.

The young prophet Samuel was awakened at night by God calling his name. At first, he thought the Priest was calling his name, but he soon discovered it was God. He responded by saying, "... Speak, for your servant is listening." (1 Samuel 3:10) God did just that. God spoke to Samuel and shared his thoughts and gave Samuel some directions. Thankfully, Samuel listened.

In another example, God spoke to Saul, "He fell to the ground and heard a voice say to him, 'Saul, Saul, why do you persecute me?' 'Who are you, Lord?' Saul asked. 'I am Jesus, whom you are persecuting,' he replied. 'Now get up and go into the city, and you will be told what you must do.'" (Acts 9:4-6) God got Saul's attention! Not only did He speak in an audible voice, He also struck Saul blind! But, importantly, when God spoke to Saul, He gave him information and directions.

Saul's story continues with God speaking to Ananias, a servant of Christ, "In Damascus there was a disciple named Ananias. The Lord called to him in a vision, 'Ananias!'" (Acts 9:10) God continues to give Ananias specific instructions of where to go and meet Saul, and what to do once he gets there. Ananias would never have gone if God had not told him to go, because at that time Saul persecuted Christians.

Throughout scripture we see that God speaks to us in many different ways: His voice, dreams, visions, and finally through His prophets. But we are deaf to His voice, unless we are listening for him. If you wait for him to strike you blind, like he did Saul, that may never happen. For most people, God speaks through dreams, visions, or in a gentle whisper, almost like a thought in your mind.

God told the prophet Elijah, "Go out and stand on the mountain in the presence of the Lord, for the Lord is about to pass by." (1 Kings 19:11) Then Elijah witnessed, ".... A great and powerful wind tore the mountains apart and shattered the rocks before the Lord, but the Lord was not in the wind. After the wind there was an earthquake, but the Lord was not in the earthquake. After the earthquake came a fire, but the Lord was not in the fire. And after the fire came a gentle whisper. When Elijah heard it, he pulled his cloak over his face and went out and stood at the mouth of the cave. Then the voice said to him..." (1 Kings 19:11-13) God spoke, but Elijah had to wait and listen for His voice. It would have been easy to be distracted by all of the big, grand events. But Elijah knew he had to wait for the voice of God.

Jesus told us, "Whoever belongs to God hears what God says. The reason you do not hear is that you do not belong to God." (John 8:47) Jesus also said, "My sheep hear my voice, and I know them, and they follow me..."

(John 10:27-28) Like a sheep knows the voice of the shepherd, we must train our ears to know the voice of God. Hearing from God and knowing His voice is something that becomes easier the closer you get to God.

God does speak today, just as He did throughout time, as seen in the Bible. God said, "I the Lord do not change…" (Malachi 3:6) God continues to lead and guide His people with His words in the Bible, through His prophets, and by speaking to us.

TEST THE SPIRITS

Imagine you are a WWI soldier who is in charge of listening to the radio to receive the orders from your General. But the enemy also has access to those same radio waves and is sending you false information, pretending to be your General. How do you know what is true information and what is from the enemy? You must be well versed in the way the General speaks, and also have some way to confirm it is him.

As you stop to yield and listen for God, how can you be sure you are hearing from God and not something else? Your own spirit has a constant stream of thoughts. There are also many spiritual beings speaking in the spirit realm: God, angels, Satan, and demons.

The truth is you may already be hearing God's voice or fighting off thoughts from demons. You may perceive it all as simply your own thoughts. Learning how to separate what are your thoughts, what is the voice of God, and what is the voice of the enemy is crucial in becoming a Prepared Warrior. If you think of the spirit realm as similar to radio waves, you need to tune into God's station.

Connecting with every spirit who whispers in your ear is unwise and dangerous. Thankfully, the Bible tells us how to test the spirits:

> *Dear friends, do not believe every spirit, but test the spirits to see whether they are from God, because many false prophets have gone out into the world. This is how you can recognize the Spirit of God: Every spirit that acknowledges that Jesus Christ has come in the flesh is from God, but every spirit that does not acknowledge Jesus is not from God. This is the spirit of the antichrist, which you have heard is coming and even now is already in the world. - 1 John 4:1-3*

As a child of God, you have authority over the spirits around you. You can command evil spirits to go, and invite the Holy Spirit in. There's a simple prayer to help you clear the atmosphere before you wait and listen for God's voice.

PRAY OUT LOUD

YIELD: In the name of Jesus Christ, my Savior, I command all evil spirits to go! God, silence the voice of the enemy, and any voice that does not declare that Jesus is Lord. Silence my own thoughts and help me to tune in to hear your voice, and yours alone. Speak Lord, your servant is listening....

As you tune into God's station, wait and listen, and keep a journal to write down what you hear or see. Don't question it at first, just watch, listen, and write. Whatever God says, write it. Whatever God shows you, write it. If God says nothing, and shows you nothing, that's ok. Next time you pray, do the same thing. Wait on God. Wait, watch, and listen.

Once you are done waiting on God, it is time to test the spirits again. If you heard something, ask God, "Jesus was I hearing your voice, the voice of the enemy, or my own thoughts?" Wait and listen again.

When you hear from God, it will always, always align with His word in the Bible. God will confirm His love for you. His character, His word, and His great love for you will be poured out to you. The fruit of the Spirit of God is evident in His words: love, joy, peace, patience, kindness, goodness, faithfulness, gentleness, and self-control. His Spirit, His speech is always in line with who He is. Get to know God through His Word in the Bible, so you can recognize His words when He speaks to you.

****** **IMPORTANT** ********

If you hear something counter to the word of God, it is not from God. God does not contradict himself. He does not want you to start a new religion. God will not tell you to murder someone. God will not tell you to commit adultery. God will not tell you that Jesus isn't the Messiah. If you hear something counter to the word of God, it is a clear sign you are hearing from an evil spirit. This is why it is essential to know the Word of God inside and out, and to pray and ask God to help you, so you won't be deceived.

Though the above warning is important, don't let it keep you from waiting to hear from God. The reality is your thoughts are just as receptive to the voice of the enemy. It's an important skill to learn how to identify the voices you hear. Any thoughts you have aligning with the character and word of God, keep.

Any thoughts you have countering the character and word of God, cast them out! Don't agree with them. Don't agree with fear or anxiety. Don't agree with murder or suicide. Don't agree with lust or greed. Though those may be your own "sin nature" thoughts, they may also be weapons of the enemy. It is wise to, "... demolish arguments and every pretension that sets itself up against the knowledge of God, and we take captive every thought to make it obedient to Christ." (2 Corinthians 10:5) Your thoughts, your prayers, your inner dialogue is like a beautiful garden you tend. Don't let the weeds grow amongst your flowers.

Praise - Repent - Ask - Yield

The beauty of a well thought out prayer time is that it honors God. God loves to hear your praise and thanksgiving. Spiritually cleansing yourself before moving forward in prayer, honors God, and the sacrifice of Jesus's death. Asking God for your requests, acknowledging His will is always above your own, honors God. Having faith that God can grant your requests, honors God. Then yielding before the King, to wait on Him, listening for his still small voice, honors God.

You may not always have the time or setting to meet with God in this prayer format. Go ahead and pray. Start communicating with God. But, when you truly come to meet with God, to connect with Him, this prayer format is a beautiful way to honor God throughout your prayer.

GOD ANSWERS PRAYER

God is alive and active in the world today. The Bible tells us, "For the eyes of the Lord are on the righteous and his ears are attentive to their prayer..." (1 Peter 3:12) God hears your prayers, and God loves to answer your prayers. James 1:17 says, "Every good and perfect gift is from above, coming down from the Father of the heavenly lights, who does not change like shifting shadows." God has perfect gifts in store for you.

Imagine a boy who goes to his father day after day to ask for a toy he wants. If the father never responds to the boy, and never gets him the toy, the boy will eventually stop coming to the father, and go ask someone else. Now imagine if that same boy went to his father and asked him for a toy. The boy said, "Dad I want a toy car, but I trust you to get me something wonderful." How delightful for the father to find just the right gift for his son.

God is the good Father who loves to give His children good gifts. Jesus said, "Which of you fathers, if your son asks for a fish, will give him a snake instead? Or if he asks for an egg, will give him a scorpion? If you then, though you are evil, know how to give good gifts to your children, how much more will your Father in heaven give the Holy Spirit to those who ask him!" (Luke 11:11-13) The amazing gift in this scripture is the Holy Spirit. But this is also a great example of how God knows what is best for us. He knows what we need, and He's not going to give us something awful. You won't be disappointed by God's gifts.

God doesn't just answer your prayers, He helps you pray, and answers them in the best ways. The Bible says, "… the Spirit helps us in our weakness. We do not know what we ought to pray for, but the Spirit himself intercedes for us through wordless groans. And he who searches our hearts knows the mind of the Spirit, because the Spirit intercedes for God's people in accordance with the will of God. And we know that in all things God works for the good of those who love him, who have been called according to his purpose." (Romans 8:26-28)

That scripture is so amazing! It tells us, the Spirit of God, like a loving father, is with you when you pray. He searches your heart and intercedes for you, with prayers in alignment with God's will! God helps you pray. It's not just up to you to say all the right words to get God to answer your prayers. God sees you where you're at. He is helping you along. He is working it all for good.

When I pray, you answer me; you encourage me by giving me the strength I need. - Psalms 138:3

PRAYER CONNECTION

Prayer Connection is much more than simply dropping off your shopping list to God. Prayer Connection is truly coming before God in an earnest desire to meet with Him, and to hear from Him. Prayer Connection is seeking God, to spend time with God. Jesus gave us wonderful examples of praying to truly meet with God. He met with the Father in prayer on a regular basis and most especially in his time of despair.

Your prayers are important to God. He collects them before His throne in heaven. God is waiting to meet with you. He listens and draws near you when you pray. So, enter into prayer with praise and thanksgiving. Honor God with your repentance and forgiveness. Seek His will to be done and have faith it will be accomplished. Then, sit quietly before the Lord, patience and open to His direction. Prayer Connection is the communication in your relationship with God. Honor God with regular prayer meetings.

TAKE ACTION

Today is a great day to start Praying. There is no need to wait for the perfect time, or the perfect place, or the perfect circumstances. Start now! There will always be a reason why you can't. Let's talk about how you can.

- Pray first thing in the morning
- Pray on your way to work or school
- Prayer walk over your work or school break
- Pray before you go to bed
- Find prayer warriors and pray with them (this is training)
- Make prayer cards to help you remember your steps
- Find scriptures to help you praise God
- Read the book of Psalms and see how David praised and thanked God

Just get started. You can refine the process later.

NOTE: The devil will try to come against you when you start to pray. Be prepared to withstand His attacks, of discouragement, busyness, etc. Plan now to NEVER GIVE UP!

PART 7

FINAL REVIEW

Chapter 25

TJ'S STORY
THE FRUIT OF FAITHFULNESS

It's hard to believe a year has gone by since TJ started attending church. But as he looked back so much had changed in his life. He went from sleepless nights, to victory after victory. Sure, TJ still had troubles, and it seemed like he was constantly praying about something. But TJ didn't feel like he was drowning anymore. No, in fact he had joy even when he shouldn't.

He felt like a completely different person from a year ago. It all started when he accepted Jesus and learned how to truly connect with God through His Word, worship and prayer. Then things really opened up when he chose to forgive his dad. After that, piece by piece, God began to work on his heart. He didn't even realize how much junk he was storing up in there. If God hadn't turned him around, he could have gotten much worse! He shot up a prayer of thanks, as was his habit now, "Thank you God for rescuing me from myself!"

Today TJ was meeting Teyo at a homeless shelter to serve meals. Again, TJ shook his head in amazement. Just one year ago it wouldn't have even crossed his mind to do something like that. He was too busy taking care of himself and his own needs. But now, TJ looked forward to serving the homeless in their community, and spreading joy and love to everyone who came in.

TJ made some new friends since last year. He started attending the youth group and found some friends who loved Jesus and tried to live according to His word. That didn't mean they were perfect. But, when they did wrong, they would apologize and talk things out. It was so great to have friends who were accountable to God. It really helped to see how he needed to grow in those areas too.

TJ's mom started attending church with him as well. Shortly after, she gave her life to Christ too! What an amazing day that was! She was also able to forgive and move past the hurts in her life. It's like a huge weight was lifted off of her. She is so much happier now. She listens to Christian music and sings as she does chores. Their whole house feels so peaceful now.

All in all, this year had totally transformed TJ's life. It was hard to imagine anything positive in his future before, if he had continued life as it was. He's so thankful God didn't give up on him or forget about him. He knew he was a beloved child.

Chapter 26

FINAL REVIEW

This book was not intended to be a quick, light read. With each section, and each chapter there were big topics to consider, and life changing decisions to make. You were challenged on every page of this book to evaluate your own understanding of who God is and your relationship with Him. You were compelled to take a clear and honest look at your own Core connection and evaluate and adjust where the Holy Spirit directed. This was not an easy book to complete. It was not for the faint of heart. It took fortitude, sincere desire for growth, and humility to endure the poking and prodding throughout this book.

You made it to this point in the book; you have the tools and knowledge within you to become a Prepared Warrior. Much like a soldier who prepares for battle, the training process is grueling. But for those who are willing to keep at it and not quit, the rewards are great.

A soldier finishes training and emerges a strong confident warrior, ready for battle. His/her body is strong, fit and ready to endure difficult terrain for hours and days on end. The soldier's mind is focused and sharp with knowledge and information ready for use. The soldier is mentally strong, not willing to be easily broken by difficult situations, or attacks by the enemy. Soldiers are trained and ready.

Are you trained and ready? As you read this book, how did you do in each section? Did you allow God to do a deep dive into your soul, or did you skip through it without introspection? Now is the time for your review. Don't shortchange yourself, skimming through the process, then be unprepared during battle. Take every step to prepare a firm foundation. Then, utilize every method of connection for meeting with God. Take every spiritual key and advance your growth quickly. These are not the days to sit on the sidelines and hope you will gather information as you go through your busy life.

Battles are raging worldwide, in the physical and spiritual realms, traumatically affecting us mentally and emotionally. This book is designed to help you quickly prepare for war, with a focus on the first principle in warfare: **Connect to the Core before you go to war**. This principle alone holds victory.

REVIEW

Let's review your training. Honestly evaluate yourself with the help of the Holy Spirit. See where you excel, where God is pleased with your knowledge and obedience. Also note where you fall short. These are areas where you need to ask God for help and guidance. Take notes and keep track as we go. Your notes will make a great prayer strategy for your prayer time.

MASTERS & ALLEGIANCE

There are clearly defined sides in spiritual battle. Jesus said, "Whoever is not with me is against me, and whoever does not gather with me scatters." (Luke 11:23)

Are you with Jesus or against Him?

Did you surrender control and acknowledge that He is Lord and Master over your life?

Ask God to clearly reveal your allegiance.

PREPARED WARRIORS

Spiritual warfare is reality. You are under attack whether you acknowledge it or not. But God is a warrior! He fights for us!

Have you committed to NEVER GIVE UP?

Will you persevere when things get rough?

Will you choose faith instead of fear?

Are you prepared for death?

Are you prepared for Christ's Return and Judgment Day?

Ask God to show you any blind spots you may have.

CORE CONNECTION

Your Core connection is the most important thing in this life and the afterlife. Your relationship with God will determine how you make it through life's battles. Your relationship with God will determine if you enter into heaven or hell. Connecting to God is the first principle in spiritual warfare.

Do you understand who God is?

Do you know God well?

Does God know you?

How much spiritual energy do you have?

Have you established a meeting time/place with God?

Are you prepared to release things to God?

Are you prepared to receive things from God?

As God to help you establish a constant Core connection.

WORD CONNECTION

The Word of God is the most reliable way to know God. God's word is Holy, trustworthy, and full of truth and wisdom. Connecting with God through His Word is the first of three methods to meet with God.

Do you read God's Word?

Do you enjoy reading God's Word or is it a task?

Do you receive anything from God when you read His Word?

Ask God to meet with you when you read His word. Be ready to release and receive as you read His Word.

WORSHIP CONNECTION

Worship is a part of the kingdom of God. Worship is a wonderful way to connect with God. All those who love God are called to worship Him. Everyone worships something or someone.

Who do you worship?

Are you embarrassed by worship or do you love it?

Do you connect with God during worship?

Have you sought out Throne Room Worship and Upward Worship songs?

Do you start your worship with praise?

Do you understand the difference between praising God and thanking God?

Can you do both or are you uncomfortable with one?

Do you receive anything from God when you worship?

Ask God to meet with you when you worship Him. Be ready to release and receive as you worship.

PRAYER CONNECTION

Prayer connects us to God in an amazing way. We communicate with God simply through speaking or thinking. It's amazing, but God actually listens to you and speaks to you. Jesus used prayer to communicate with God the Father while He was here on earth.

Do you pray to God?

Do you enjoy praying or is it boring to you?

Do you start our prayers with praise?

When the Holy Spirit convicts you of sin, do you repent?

Are you holding any unforgiveness in your heart?

When you ask God for something, do you believe He will do it for you?

Do you believe God can do it? Do you ask God for small things?

Do you trust that God's will is best?

Are you persistent with your prayers or do you lose hope?

Have you practiced waiting on the Lord?

How long did you wait? Do you believe God can and will speak to you?

Do you believe God answers prayers?

Ask God to meet with you when you pray. Be ready to release and receive as you pray.

THE CORE

Chapter 36

GET READY. STAY READY.

Now that we have reviewed each section, you have a better view of your spiritual state. How prepared are you spiritually? Are you just beginning? Are you halfway there? Or, are you advanced in the process? Wherever you are, that's a perfect place to start. No one is perfect, or 100% prepared. This is an ongoing and whole life process. Take the information you have learned here and put it into practice on a day-to-day basis. Your daily training begins now.

To be a successful warrior, you must learn, train, and make preparations. You can't expect to skip over or ignore training and hope to be successful on the battlefield. If you never pick up a gun before engaging in a gunfight, your chances of coming out alive are very slim. Likewise, we must prepare for spiritual battles, because like it or not, we are all being actively attacked by the enemy, and likely on many fronts.

Daily Core connection is your day-to-day training. The more regularly you connect to the Core, the easier it will become. It will become as customary as brushing your teeth each day. Your day will not be complete without meeting with God. The regularity of your meetings with God will always strengthen your relationship with God.

God will help you grow. God will help you learn. God will direct you. Your faith in God will grow. Then, one day, without warning, you will take a look at yourself and realize, you have become what God created you to be, a Prepared Warrior.

A successful soldier knows how to get ready and stay ready. A soldier doesn't just train and prepare then take the next few years off. Soldiers get ready, then maintain their training and discipline to ensure that the day battle comes, they are prepared to fight.

Commit to the process until you see results. You don't stop working out after your first session, or you will never see results. You may start off awkward and out of shape. But, if you keep working out, one day you will see more muscle definition, your pants will fit better, people will start to notice it too. They will ask what you've been doing, so they can try it themselves. You won't feel right about missing your workout, because now that's part of who you are.

It is the same thing with the Core connection, keep connecting until you see results. Don't stop connecting to God after your first few times. You may feel awkward and unsure. But if you keep connecting, then one day you'll realize how much more peace you have, you don't let things get to you anymore, people will start to notice a change too. They will see something has changed in you, and desire what you have. You won't feel right about missing your time with God, because it's such an important part of who you are.

CLOSING

As Prepared Warriors, we spiritually prepare for life's battles and judgment day. The first step is Core connection. Connecting with God on a daily basis through His Word, Worship and Prayer. No matter what battle you face, meeting with God and spending time in His presence is always the right answer. He is your source for peace, love, joy, relationship, acceptance, purpose and more. He is your Father, your healer, your provider, your best friend. He has infinite wisdom, knowledge and power. His is the ultimate power and authority. The closer you get to God the better. Life will never be easy, but with God you will endure, persevere and never give up.

May you boldly share Jesus Christ with those who do not know Him, even if they profess a different religion. As you become a Prepared Warrior, may you share these truths with all those around you, until you are surrounded by Prepared Warriors. May you and your family be prepared for life's battles and judgment day.

REFERENCE LIST

All Scripture quotations, unless otherwise indicated, are taken from the Holy Bible, New International Version®, NIV®. Copyright ©1973, 1978, 1984, 2011 by Biblica, Inc.™ Used by permission of Zondervan. All rights reserved worldwide. www.zondervan.com The "NIV" and "New International Version" are trademarks registered in the United States Patent and Trademark Office by Biblica, Inc.™ Book "Science Speaks" by Peter W. Stoner, M.S. and Robert C. Newman, S.T.M., Ph.D.

Connor, Bobby. Preacher. Lancaster Prophetic Conference. August 2018.

"Core." *Merriam-Webster.com*. 2020. https://www.merriam-webster.com (10 May 2020).

Miller, Bud and Betty. "What the Bible Says about Spiritually Cleansing Your Home." *Bibleresources.com*. May 2020. https://bibleresources.org/spiritually-cleansing-home/

Murdock, Stan. Retired Pastor. First Baptist Church of Kearney, Nebraska.

Selvaraj, Sadhu Sundar. Prophet. Lancaster Prophetic Conference. August 2018.

Stoner, Peter. Science Speaks. Moody Books Press (3rd Revised Edition), 1969.

Tzu, Sun. The Art of War. English translation by Lionel Giles, M.A. 1910.

Made in USA - Kendallville, IN
1162788_9781735561806
09.10.2020 0951